10·8·18

Amy.
May you find God at
work in your story, Johns:17,
and may you be delighted by
the ways in which God
turns current ashes into
future beauty!
With hope—
Kate

I Am Unique

There is no one to compare myself to and no one to compete with. When I know that I am doing my very best, I am satisfied. All notions of "better" or "worse" dissolve. When I come in contact with others, I can admire their beauty and wisdom without diminishing my own.

For years I have wished for a different body, a different personality, different life. Now I know what a waste of time this is. I awaken to my inner beauty, and I realize my own magnificence.

Today I clearly see that there is no one to compete with—there never was. When the orchid and the rose are side by side, is one more perfect than the other?

In recovery, I am coming to see how extraordinary and incomparable I am. My interactions with others will be free from any thought of competition.

Daily Affirmations
Rokelle Lerner

A Craving for Life

KATE SULLIVAN WATKINS

HILLSBORO PRESS
Franklin, Tennessee

Printed in the United States of America

99   98   97   96   95   6   5   4   3   2   1

Library of Congress Catalog Card Number: 95-78617

ISBN: 1-881576-63-9

The poem, "Please Hear What I'm Not Saying," used by permission of the author Charles C. Finn, © 1966.

Published by
HILLSBORO PRESS
an imprint of
PROVIDENCE HOUSE PUBLISHERS
P.O. Box 158 • 238 Seaboard Lane
Franklin, Tennessee 37067
800-321-5692

To Larry—thank you for your strong hands when I was too weak to stand, your warm heart when I was too cold to feel, and your fresh ham sandwiches when I was desperate to survive. I love you.

and

To Baker and Molly Katherine—the love in your eyes is strong enough to move mountains. Thank you for your laughter, your gentle touches, and your childlike kindness. May you always realize how special God made you. I love you. Mom.

Contents

Foreword

*M*y ninety-three-year-old grandmother knew her only from the snapshot in the tiny mosaic frame on a shelf of her nursing-home room. She called her *Beautiful Kate*. I recall the look of pride in her father's face January 10, 1967, when I told him we had a little girl. "I know, Darlin'," he beamed.

Growing up, she was both a tomboy and a little lady. She loved to wear rings on all her fingers and carried a purse chock-full of little girl treasures. She would follow her older brothers down to the creek, fight for play space under the limbs of the 150-year-old pecan tree that was both their sandbox and swing set, and pick spring buttercups for her mom.

When the boys were at school, she would run errands with me and soon learned the location of every gumball machine in town. At home, she would line up her dolls and stuffed animals, get out the picture books, and sit for hours "reading" to her willing "students."

She began school eagerly. In third grade she wanted to read aloud to her classmates after lunch, but they weren't always as willing to listen as her stuffed teddy bears. The next year, she was wearing a shirt loudly proclaiming herself *Kate the Great*. At a class picnic, she could beat the boys in a mud-wrestling contest. In junior high, she once grabbed a boy's gold neckchain, twisting it fiercely when he made a derogatory remark in her direction. With her brothers' help, she learned to wrangle the 1,000 pound "calves" for the annual 4-H steer shows but she would sob pitifully when her steer was led off to market. She was growing into a young lady, but she was tough. I was proud of this. Kate had the determination to be whatever she chose and would have the strength to back up the decisions in her life. What happened at age thirteen to make the girl who had it altogether on the outside crumble on the inside? Why wasn't I, as her mother, more aware of the anguish beneath the facade?

I took a full-time job at a local radio station about the same time Kate's bulimia started. I loved the job and spent many more hours away from home than I had in the past. Did the fact that I was caught up in my job prevent me from noticing what was happening in my own home?

When she started dating, Kate would come to me with details of the evening's outing. I was pleased we seemed to have the lines of communication open between us. Many mothers and daughters did not. I felt lucky. How could I know Kate was practicing selective communication with me too.

While Kate was experiencing her inner trial, she didn't let it stop her from enjoying good times with her family. The two of us would go shopping for new outfits, and once took in two movies and pizza on a Saturday when the men in the family had headed out of town to a farm equipment show. The whole family took part in the productions put on by Franklin's Pull-Tight Players and Kate and I looked forward to the Broadway shows that came to the Tennessee Performing Arts Center in Nashville.

Kate was a little girl who had it altogether. She's grown into an adult who has her priorities in the right place. She's put herself through a torment only she knows. The toughness she displayed as a youngster has helped her endure.

Her great-grandmother was right. She will always be *Beautiful Kate*.

—Lyn Sullivan Pewitt
April 1995

Preface

$\mathcal{B}$eing the only daughter and having three older brothers might be the reason. Trying to always please others first, and being a perfectionist may be why it happened. Having been born during the time that "thin was in" could be to blame. Whatever the reason, during the years that I was supposed to be young, healthy, and carefree, I learned to be dishonest, deceptive, and out of control.

That is what happens when one has an eating disorder. Mine, bulimia, was my hidden shadow for eleven years. Even when the lights were out, it would cling to my soul. No matter how I tried, I couldn't free myself from it. It has been said that a bulimic's need to binge and purge is greater than a drug addict's need for the drug of choice.

My thoughts were constantly about food. What to eat, when to eat, and where to eat were questions that took precedence over everything else.

As I chewed, I could feel myself getting fatter. When I swallowed, I hated myself just a little bit more. As I purged, I always vowed to never do it again.

Violent purging was an attempt to release all of the things that I had no control over. A release of pain and fears. I was struggling to be someone, something other than who or what I had become. The cycle was vicious.

I would try to control my weight in a useless effort to control my life. Ultimately, losing weight didn't please me. I would starve to lose more, and the need for food would overcome me. I would binge on thousands of calories within a matter of minutes, and purge to keep from putting on more weight. Daily for years, my mind was at odds with my body. I was slowly losing the struggle. This is my very personal and honest story.

In writing this book, I have changed some names and left out some important events. My intent is not to hurt those that I know, but to help those that I do not. I hope that my story helps you.

Acknowledgments

*G*od—My winding path has always led me back to You. Thank You for surrounding me with people who were willing to help me battle my illness. Thank You for loving me when I couldn't love myself. I know that You understood my pain in my darkest moments.

Mom—You have tremendous strength. I admire your willingness to experience the unknown. Thank you for your incredible support with my recovery, my story, and my life.

Perfect Daddy—Thank you for always being there to make me feel safe. I never realized how much I treasured your laughter and your love until you were gone. I miss you.

Jim, Mike, and Pat—Thank you for sharing your childhoods with me. We were a great team.

Zack and Zeke—Thank you for welcoming me into your wonderful family. Zack, your gentleness will warm many hearts. Zeke, your creativity is a true gift. I know that you will use it wisely.

William S. Marley—You were able to see my dreams behind my shield. Thank you for reaching out and prompting me in the right direction. Your belief in me gave me courage.

Judy Jackson—Your incredible teaching gift was a pleasure for me to experience. Thank you for being so patient and willing to share your knowledge as well as your friendship.

Fritz and Jane Gilbert—Thank you for convincing me that my story was worth telling.

My childhood friends—Chandy, Lisa W., Melody—your constant friendship has shared all phases of my life. Thank you for standing strong beside me. The laughter we shared and continue to share, echoes in my mind.

Suzanne and Victor—Your gentle strength is so refreshing. Thank you for letting Christ be first in your life and for sharing your kindness with my family. Your friendship is a treasure to me.

Debbie—Your honesty has been so helpful in my recovery. You help me to see things in a new light. Thank you for always listening and offering kind words.

Lisa Carson—Thank you for the generosity that you have shown my family. Your understanding of the legal system has been greatly appreciated.

Bill Peach—Thank you for leading me to Mary Bray Wheeler and Hillsboro Press at Providence House Publishers. Without you, this work would still be in a drawer.

Andy Miller, Mary Bray Wheeler, Jo Jaworski, Charlie Flood, Trinda Cole, Judy Coursey, and Holly Jones—Thank you for seeing potential in my story for your Hillsboro Press imprint. Your hard work and warm smiles have made this project a joy.

David W. McMillan, Ph.D., and Gerre White, L.C.S.W., of the Park West Eating Disorders program in Nashville, Tennessee—Your willingness to professionally review my story is an affirmation of your dedication. Thank you for being my gateway to the recovery process.

Charles Finn—Thank you for trusting me with your masterpiece.

Tamara—God blessed you with the ability to understand my heart. Your health is so important. Always realize that you are too. Thank you for caring enough to live. You truly understand.

And finally, thank you to all those who have reached out to me and shared your story. God bless you; there is hope.

Chapter 1

The Only Girl

*D*addy, why do some cows have larger udders than others?" I asked my father as we rode the horses around our family farm. "They are like women," he said, "some are larger than others." My brothers chuckled at his response.

I'll never know if my father's answer was directed at me. I do know that the sound of his voice still rings in my head, and I can still see the smile on his face.

My father was a caring man. He was the oldest of five children, and stories are told about his willfulness from a very early age. Being reared on a farm, he learned quickly that strength and hard work were the tools needed to survive. As a teenager, he was left in charge of the family and farm while his father fought overseas.

Caring describes my father; understanding doesn't. It was never questioned who was in charge of our family. If one of his children disagreed with his opinion, they were not encouraged to discuss that with him. When my father and I did have different ideas, the words "disrespectful, back-talking, sassing, little girl, and spanking," could be heard coming from his mouth. I learned as a young child to swallow my anger and pride. Going head on with my father only got me into more trouble. It was easier to just agree than to face the consequences of disagreeing. As years and arguments passed, my pain and need for expression got shoved deeper within myself.

My mother worked inside the home until I was twelve years old. She was always the first mother at the school parties and the last one to leave. She was a homemaker, charity volunteer, and head driver to baseball games and skating parties. She knew how to throw the best slumber parties in town and was a master at selling Girl Scout

Cookies. On a farm, there was always plenty for the "woman of the house" to do. Feeding a family of six, cleaning, and canning kept her quite busy. She taught me the secret of family recipes and how to scrub a commode correctly. She never knew how important these lessons would become to me.

Mom was an energetic mother but a submissive wife. I have seen her bounce around the room singing, but the silence would become deafening when she and Daddy would argue. This didn't happen often, but when it did, they would go days without talking. Their children would become their messengers, and cold suppers made a loud statement. My brothers and I would tiptoe around the house trying to avoid any conflicts. I thought that it was my job to try and "fix" things. I would try to explain things to my mother and then to my father. All of my coaxing was useless, but I gave it all I had.

Being the youngest and the only daughter did have its advantages. I'll be the first to admit that when it came to getting my way, I won hands down in comparison to my brothers. I usually won the arguments with my brothers when my parents intervened. I was the only one who had my own bathroom. I needed the largest closet. Basically, I was spoiled rotten.

As a child I was never physically abused. I never lacked for any material needs. I can't recall any horrible events that happened in my life. To the unsuspecting viewer, it seemed that my life was completely normal. However, at the innocent age of thirteen, something went terribly wrong.

Chapter 2

An Innocent Beginning

As a teenager, I became active in my church youth group. I was close to my youth director and felt like we had a special friendship. He was a young married man and the father of a small boy. His wife was diligent in working with the church, and her ideas were innovative. Sunday nights were spent making super-size sub sandwiches, playing silly games, and learning about the Lord. This young, exciting family was a hit with the teenagers.

Dana and I had been friends since kindergarten. She also enjoyed the company of Mark and his wife and child. Their door was always open, and we began to take advantage of their hospitality. They were living in a house that the church had provided them. We would help them clean their yard, take care of their child, and prepare for Sunday devotionals.

When one is thirteen, it is important to find a place to fit in and feel accepted. We thought they needed us, and we knew we needed them.

Mark started asking Dana and I to spend the night at their house. We would share a family dinner, and then enjoy each other's company. After his wife and child would go to bed, Mark would come up to our room. Dana and I would sit on the bed in our T-shirts, and Mark would sit on the floor. We would talk for hours, sometimes even until the sun was on the way back up again. Neither of us were used to men who were so open about their emotions. It was a refreshing change.

Being young and naive, we would tell our parents about our visit. They felt uncomfortable with the situation and decided that it wasn't appropriate. Appropriate or not, we were allowed to spend the night again.

Mark was offered another job out of state. We were all aware that he and his family would have to move. Dana and I were especially upset. Mark asked us to spend the night one last time before the moving van came and the boxes were loaded.

It was Father's Day weekend, and I asked for my parent's permission. Permission denied. Mom made wonderful excuses that we all needed to be together as a family. She had purchased an ice cream cake in the shape of a coat and tie to celebrate the holiday. We were going to have "quality family time." I explained to my parents how important that it was for me to sleep over one more time. Permission denied.

I decided that if I couldn't spend the night, I wasn't about to celebrate with my family. I knew that I loved my dad, and I was thankful for him. However, I didn't want to smile and act like I wasn't angry. While my family celebrated, I sulked in the privacy of my bedroom.

After school on Monday, I began to think about that cake. After all, I did love ice-cream cake, and it was a rarity. If I ate it without my family, it wouldn't be as if I were celebrating with them. No one was home, so as I opened the refrigerator, I decided to cut myself a large piece. It was mint chocolate-chip ice cream with chocolate cake. My mouth watered as the knife slid down through the ice cream and then the cake. What a treat!

My plate was empty within minutes. I returned to the kitchen and cut myself a larger piece. As I ate, the conflict with my parents played over and over in my mind. Why couldn't I go? Why couldn't I go? Empty plate, more cake. I can't believe I couldn't go. Didn't they have any regard for my feelings?

When my plate was empty for the fourth time, I began to panic. I had eaten almost all of what was left of the cake. I thought it odd that after the first piece, I hadn't really noticed how it had tasted in my mouth nor when I swallowed. I had just been shoveling it in.

I knew that I had two problems that needed to be answered quickly. How did I plan to explain to my family where all of the dessert had gone? It had only been in our house for twenty-four hours, and it was almost completely wiped out.

I was also aware that I had consumed many more calories than a body needed. Especially mine since I was already overweight. My brothers never missed an opportunity to point that out to me. Four large pieces of ice cream cake. Supper would be served in a few hours. How could I eat again?

As the panic spread over me, so did the solution. I walked up the cold hall in my bare feet. As I opened the bathroom door, I glared at the commode. That was my answer. Whenever I got sick, I would lose weight because I would throw up. That's what I had to do now. I had to throw up.

I got down on my knees and lifted the lid. Drops of dried urine were around the rim where the males in my house had missed their target. With one hand I pulled my long hair out of my face. Using the other hand I forced two fingers down my throat. What a terrible feeling. I could feel the "treat" as it exited my stomach and entered my esophagus. Within seconds it was filling my mouth and splashing into the commode. What was so wonderful minutes ago was now repulsive. After heaving violently several times, I felt like the job was complete. I cleaned up the inside of the commode, flushed, and put the lid back down. I splashed my face with cold water and blew my nose. In the white toilet paper, I noticed pieces of cake that had come out of my nose. I was disgusted by my actions, but felt relief knowing that my splurge wouldn't make me any fatter. As I left the bathroom, I turned out the light; everything looked exactly as it had before.

At supper that night no one asked about the cake. With six people in the family, food didn't last long anyway.

As I lay in bed with only the hall night light illuminating the room, I was proud of myself. I didn't know where the idea to purge had come from, but I knew that it had worked. I had eaten as much cake as I wanted but I didn't have to suffer the consequences. I thought I had been so clever. What I didn't know was that I had had my first experience with a disease that would one day threaten my very life.

Chapter 3

Dangerous Secrets

I was always a good student in school. When I was in the fourth grade, I completed a project that was to be turned in a month later in one night. Procrastination was never my style. While maintaining an A, B average in junior-high, I was a member of the student council, the band, and a small theatrical group.

Like most thirteen-year-old girls, my friends were important to me. As I began to physically develop, I noticed that I was larger than most of them. I had trouble finding bras that fit me correctly, so wrinkles could always be seen under my shirts. I was self-conscious about my appearance and developed the habit of keeping my arms up around my chest to try and conceal my breasts and wrinkles.

Since laughter always makes everyone seem comfortable, I would use it to lessen my own pain. At lunch, my friends would joke that I was the only one who could rest my breasts on the table while I ate. They were right. Although this embarrassed me, I would laugh along with everyone else. As I became increasingly concerned about my weight, I started bringing salads for lunch. There were no salad bars in our cafeteria, so keeping a salad fresh and tasty until noon was hard to do. I thought that a soggy green salad was worth suffering through if the end result would be a smaller me.

I started my menstrual cycle during that year. It is such an uncertain time for young teenage girls. They are concerned that they will be "caught" without the proper supplies, and everyone in school will notice a blood stain on their pants before they do. This never happened to me. My period only lasted one day. In the beginning that is normal. As one's body continues to change, a period will last from five to seven days. Until I was twenty-four years old, one day was the extent of my discomfort. What I didn't know at age thirteen was that as my body changed normally, my eating habits would change abnormally.

My best friend in the world, Chandy, was beautiful—tall and thin, the cheerleader type. Her hair was long and wavy, and "bad hair day" wasn't in her vocabulary. She had prominent cheek bones, and her teeth were perfectly straight. I felt that when I stood beside her, my common but large features increased her beauty. If a boy became friends with me, it was usually to get to know Chandy. I was always the buddy and she was always the girlfriend. She wasn't the most popular girl in the school, but I sure wanted to be like her.

Whenever my mother would take me shopping, I would constantly hold up clothes and say, "This would look great on Chandy." For a while Mom would ignore me. Then, she would glare at me and say, "We're not shopping for Chandy. We're shopping for you." I never thought things looked good on me. Trying to improve my looks was just a waste of time. Eventually, I had my hair cut like hers. I wore my makeup the way she taught me to, and the clothes that I did buy were like things that she already owned.

Chandy never knew that I idolized her. I acted like the latest fashions and flashy makeup were not important to me. If I couldn't be beautiful, I discovered that I could be funny.

Laughter became a wall that I built around my insecure self. If people were bent over laughing, they wouldn't take time to notice my crooked teeth and wide hips. I was easily fooling a lot of people.

One person that I wasn't fooling was myself. Purging the ice cream cake had seemed like a positive experience for me. Binging and purging was becoming habit-forming. I had no idea that in my quest for perfection, my thoughts and actions were becoming dangerous.

I began to skip lunch at school, then tell my parents that I wasn't hungry for supper because I had eaten a large lunch. I was never a breakfast eater, so I was going all day without eating a thing. I would be ravenous by bedtime.

I wanted to lose weight, but I was unable to sleep with the pains that were shooting in my stomach. While others were asleep or watching television, I would quietly sneak into the kitchen.

Our house was always stocked with junk food. We usually had three different kinds of Little Debbie treats, numerous bags of chips, and enough flavors of ice cream to make a rainbow.

Once I would begin to eat, I was unable to stop. I got so wrapped up in what I was eating that I would shove food in faster and faster. The taste began to disappear as my stomach grew more and more distended. I would eat until I was literally uncomfortable walking. I then felt that the only choice I had was to purge in my own tiny bathroom. Since my bathroom could only be entered through my room, I felt relatively sure that no one would discover me as I rid myself of my nightly binge.

If I did sit down and enjoy dinner and conversation with my family, I would usually excuse myself immediately after my last bite had been swallowed. I had a variety of reasons for leaving so quickly. They ranged from homework that needed completing, friends that needed calling, and things that needed cleaning. There was only one real reason for my exit. I was on my way to regurgitate all that my mom had just recently prepared to provide her family with nutrition.

With my head resting on my mother's lap one Friday night, we started watching 20/20. Hugh Downs held up a chart and explained a new disorder that doctors were researching. It was called bulimia. He went on to detail symptoms that included eating large quantities of food and purging to get it out of one's system. He was descriptive about how the lining of one's esophagus could be torn because of stomach acid slowly eroding the tissue away. He talked about swollen saliva glands and decaying teeth.

As my family watched unsuspectingly, I began to worry. Was he describing what I had been doing? Was it true that there are other people who were doing exactly what I was? Where did they get the idea? Does this thing have a real name? A wash of questions began to fill my mind. I didn't like the way that I looked, but I certainly didn't want to hurt myself. Boy, would my parents be mad then. Within myself, I decided that I had thrown up for the last time.

A few days later, I got up the nerve to tell Chandy what I had been doing. I told her that I had only done it a few times, and that I wasn't ever going to do it again. I didn't know at that time that I had just told the first of many lies. "Please don't tell anyone." I said.

"Don't worry, I don't want people to think I have a best friend that's crazy," she laughed. Chandy never did tell, but she had no idea what a dangerous secret she was keeping.

I thought I was finished with my tricks. I planned to eat a regular lunch, and get back on schedule with supper. I thought I could simply stop. After all, I had something with a "name" that could hurt me. I assumed I had control over my own actions, and certainly my own body. I was wrong; my disease with a name, bulimia, already had control of me. My struggle was not ending, but just beginning.

Chapter 4

It's Never Enough

On a farm, there was never a shortage of chores that needed to be done. In my home, the women worked inside, and the men kept the fields in order. Several times, I tried to carry my weight along with my brothers. I always failed. I could open gates, but castrating calves and hauling hay was not for me. I decided that my place was in the kitchen beside my mother.

During the summer months, I was in charge of cleaning and cooking lunch while she was at work. I liked being in charge, even if the tasks weren't glamorous.

Feeding four hungry farm hands and extra teenage helpers was not easy. I decided that I wanted them to be impressed with my cooking. Some of the helpers were cute, and I was at the age that I noticed that. I was going to have to prepare more than cold sandwiches and chips if I wanted to be noticed.

I would follow some of Mom's standard recipes, and enjoyed experimenting with new ones. Fresh squeezed lemonade became a favorite of my brothers. Although it took a lot of time, and a bushel of lemons, it was worth the compliments.

It was important for me to please, especially my father. After enjoying a batch of biscuits, he kept referring to them as "cracker jacks." I rushed in the other room, called Mom, and discovered that yes, cracker jack was a good thing.

Since the average lunch that I would prepare consisted of fried chicken, mashed potatoes, homegrown corn, and fresh bread, Mom usually made a light supper. Light at our house meant a meat and two vegetables, not three. Also, no meal was complete without a fresh pie or cake.

As a child, my homework was always completed. My room was always clean. My mind was constantly telling me that I needed to be better.

I can never remember anyone telling me, "Kate, this isn't good enough." Math was not my best subject, but my parents assumed that since I did my best in everything else, I must be going my best in it as well. I was thankful they didn't put extra pressure on top of what I was already putting on myself. I always wanted my science project to be the best. My handwriting had to be beautiful, and my notebook had to be organized. I was fighting a self-inflicted struggle, and I was loosing terribly. After I mastered "having it all together" in the class-room, it was time to work on my body. What a job that would be!

I loved to eat. Sweets were my passion. If I ever earned any money as a child, I would always spend it on candy. I would fill my hands with treats, walk up to the counter, and ask the salesperson if I had enough money. When the response was "no," it was a real chore to decide what to put back. If I was going to the store with my mother and had no money of my own, I would go into my brothers' room and look for loose change on the floor. I even discovered that coins could be found beside stale cheese puffs in the couch. I didn't think of it as stealing, simply cleaning up.

I would make my purchase while my mother was in a different part of the store. If she saw the amount of junk that I was buying, she would make me put some of it back. I had made my choices, and I wanted it all. I would keep it in my room, and eat it when no one else was around. It's strange that bad habits that I developed at age six have followed me my entire life.

Other than sweets, I could get pleasure out of just about everything else that I consumed. My brothers never missed an opportunity to point that out to me. As my breasts grew, so did my hips and thighs.

With my family, it was necessary to eat quickly if one wanted second helpings. I always did. My brothers ate fast, so I ate fast. I would base the amount of food that I ate on the amount that they ate. When they quit, I quit. At that time, society dictated that women should be fit and trim, but men didn't need to worry until they couldn't get through elevator doors. Although these standards have changed some, most men still aren't that concerned about their weight. At age thirteen, no one told me the rules. I didn't know that I wasn't supposed to eat what I wanted. This was when bulimia and I really became close. I decided that I still wanted to eat a lot. The sensation of being "full" never kept me from loading up my plate again. If I was still going to eat what I wanted, and as much as I wanted, there was only one answer. I decided to disregard the warnings of Hugh Downs and continue with my nasty habit. I had to eat without recourse. I had to purge.

There are different ways that bulimics choose to purge. Some take an exorbitant amount of laxatives. I have heard people describe how they felt after swallowing four boxes of laxatives in a single day. The side effects are uncomfortable, as well as dangerous. Chronic diarrhea causes dehydration. With a loss of body salts and minerals, muscles become weak and the heart rate becomes erratic. Ironically, with continued laxative abuse secondary constipation develops, and the sufferer is required to take even more laxatives. As with all forms of purging, it is a vicious cycle.

I experimented with laxatives on only one occasion. The two or three pills that I took made me so uncomfortable that I took several doses of Pepto Bismol to combat the diarrhea. During the night, I felt very strange. My head began to spin, and I was weaker than normal. I got out of bed, made it through my door, and collapsed on the cold tile floor of the bathroom. I lay there for several hours before I was able to wander back to bed. At the time, I was glad that I wasn't discovered. Looking back I wonder if someone had found me, would things have turned out differently? Probably not, I would have smiled and denied my problem.

Overexercising is another means of purging. Bulimics will spend hours on a treadmill or exercise bike. They might then continue with aerobics or floor work. As I began my disease, I didn't do much exercising. I tried running through the fields, but all I got were tender breasts and a sore back. I did experiment with floor work, but when the results were not immediate, I went back to vomiting.

No matter how I tried to lose weight, putting my fragile face into the stinky, moldy commode seemed the only way.

During my freshman year, I really shined as an overachiever. I was the president of the student council and I took my responsibility seriously.

We had been planning a special spirit week for the students. On Friday, there was to be an assembly of the entire student body. Different activities were planned including a drawing of names to win certain prizes. I was very sick that week. From my bed, I contacted local merchants to ask for items to be donated for our drawing. I wrote notes daily to the faculty sponsor and sent them by way of friends. I told her about different ideas that I had. The point is, I was being obsessive. I didn't think that another "well" student could get merchants to donate prizes. I didn't even trust the faculty member to get the job done without me. I liked being in control, and I thought things would fall apart if I wasn't there. I missed the assembly and everything was fine. I didn't know how they had done it without me.

At the end of the year, I was voted the "wittiest" female by my classmates. Webster's describes witty as being humorous, facetious (comical, flippant), and jocular. Maybe my theatrical work was paying off. If everyone thought that I was comical and flippant, it really didn't seem to matter what I thought. No, I wasn't voted most popular, or most likely to succeed, but gosh, I was something!

I was also selected by the faculty to receive the "citizenship" award. The student body reluctantly gathered in the gymnasium for an afternoon awards ceremony. We decided that time in the gym was better than time in the classroom. Most of the awards were for superior academic achievements. When I looked around and saw my parents, I was pretty certain that I wasn't being honored with the math award. My name was called to be recognized as "best citizen in the ninth grade." My parents were proud and in turn so was I. I jokingly told my friends, "If you can't be smart, be good."

Wow, wasn't I a great kid. I was funny, responsible, and a good citizen. What else could I be? Well, I could be taller, have prettier hair, longer nails, smaller breasts, narrower hips, and thinner thighs, just to name a few. It was hard for me to settle with simply being a funny, good citizen.

Chapter 5

Misfits and Big Boobs

Becoming a high school student is such an intimidating time in one's life. Horror stories are told about underclassmen being put in lockers and left there for the remainder of the day. Fears of not being able to locate the correct classroom are shared by all the newcomers. The amount of nightly homework is supposedly immeasurable. Although most rumors are dispelled after a few days, it's still normal for one to feel insecure.

It seems that if you're driving, someone else always has a nicer vehicle than yours. If you're in the band, someone else can play their instrument better than you can. And, even if you have an eating disorder, someone else is still thinner than you are.

As in junior high, I wasn't concerned about fashion. I liked to wear long T-shirts and over-sized sweatshirts. I thought that they were a good disguise for my large chest and expanding waistline. Jeans were usually the order of the day. Looking back, I realize that I looked plain sloppy. I didn't have a perfect figure, but I sure could have done a better job with what God had given me.

I met a very handsome "older guy" my sophomore year. Actually, he had been a friend of the family's for years, and our fathers had grown up together. He was one of the male teenagers that I would try to impress as I cooked lunch for my family during the summer. My father liked him, and once again, his approval was important.

We had gotten to know each other through church. His name was John, and I thought he was the one for me. He was already a graduate of my high school. I thought that made him even more special. In my eyes, he could have any girl he wanted. I wasn't quite sure why he had picked me.

His attire was the spitting image of my brothers. I rarely saw him in anything other than flannel shirts, Lee boot-cut jeans, and cowboy boots. I felt like he fit my mold of "the perfect man."

When we first started seeing each other, my parents preferred that we go out with friends and not alone. We would spend our weekend nights with other friends from church. After one Sunday night at the pizza place, he told me he would call me later. Well, since I'm not a procrastinator, I assume that those around me aren't either. I have discovered many times how wrong my assumption is.

I waited, but the phone didn't ring for several days. My hopes were dashed. All of my uncertainties about myself turned into complete paranoia. I decided that he hadn't called because I wasn't mature, pretty, or thin.

On Thanksgiving Day, my mother filled our home with a wonderful aroma and a lot of family. She cooked for days, and the results were always worth the wait. As I sat at the festive table, I had a hard time thinking of things to be thankful for. I was so disappointed that John had not called. I loaded up my plate with meats, vegetables, things that were pickled, and an array of sweets. Like everyone else, I emptied my plate. Food was never to be wasted. After the final crumb was gone, I excused myself from the table. With all of the company, I wasn't missed.

Hours of hard work by my mother lay in the bottom of the commode within seconds. My Thanksgiving meal was the recipient of the disappointment I felt over a phone call. John did call later, but it was too late for my meal.

I asked him in an unassuming way why he hadn't called when he had said he would. He told me that he hadn't told me when he would call, just that he would call. I felt badly that I had gotten so upset over a misinterpreted conversation.

As time passed, we found different excuses to be together. My father was concerned that we were getting "too serious too soon," but I was trying to be with him as much as I was allowed. It was comforting to never have to worry about who I would go to a dance with. My Friday nights were always booked, and I had a warm hand to hold during church. It made me feel important to know that someone wanted to spend time with me. Sometimes in life we do things for the wrong reasons.

Although I had someone special in my life, I didn't feel that I was special. I was continuing to use food to deal with excitement in my life as well as disappointment. Before a date, I would binge on things in the house, and throw them back up when others were not around. After a date, I would throw up in my bathroom when everyone else had gone to bed. Sometimes the meal had been in my stomach for hours. The acid in my stomach was doing its job to break the food down for digestion. I knew that as I purged, the repulsive remains would taste sour. I knew that the smell in the air was horrid. I also knew that the remains that took the wrong path would burn the sensitive lining in my nose. What I didn't know was that it was slowly eating away at my esophagus. Even if I had known or cared, I was too far along in my disease to know how to stop the cycle. I was thankful for a companion, yet I didn't know how to be thankful for myself.

As president of my junior class, I was in charge of the prom committee. Prom is an event that a young girl dreams about forever. It's her night to be Cinderella. With just the right dress, just the right hair, and just the right date, the evening could be magical. I thought that one out of three was not bad. It's not that I was crazy about my date; I was crazy with the thought that I had a date.

Shopping for my beautiful prom dress became a disheartening experience. I knew what I wanted to wear, but I knew that I wouldn't look good in it. I was 5'4", 140 pounds, and wore a 36FF bra. Not many women wear a 36FF, much less teenagers.

When I found a size 11 dress that I thought would be acceptable, I ventured to try it on. As it went over my head and passed my shoulders, I knew it wasn't going to work. I slowly began to zip it up. With each tooth in the zipper, it got a little tighter. It completely locked up at my waist. The zipper was stuck and it could go no further. The saleswoman said "come on out and show us how beautiful you look." Right, I had on worn-out tennis shoes, my hair was stringy, and my breasts were extended out far enough to choke a horse. May I also add that they weren't covered up. I didn't want to leave the privacy of the small dressing room, but she insisted. She thought I should stand in front of the three-way mirror. I didn't like what I saw in one mirror, why would I want to look at myself in three? I hesitantly exited from my shell.

As I walked toward the mirror and onto the platform, the saleswoman asked the lady in alterations to come help us out. As she would tug on one side of the dress, I would pop out of the other side. Why didn't we just hang this thing up and I could get a burlap sack from the barn? She kept tugging and pinning, and I kept feeling like it was hopeless. I pointed out to her that no matter how many pins she had used, my boobs were still exposed. She replied in a cheerful, southern voice, "Oh don't worry, Honey, I do alterations for Dolly Parton and her sister. I can fix this. We'll just sew in some extra material in the seams." I knew that when I looked down in this dress, I could see my cleavage line extending to my toes, but I never anticipated a response like the one she had just given me.

I wanted to crawl into a hole, bury myself along with my "Dolly Parton" breasts, and die! I couldn't believe she had just told me this. Did she think that I would be flattered? I wanted to be able to buy a size 6 dress off of the rack, and have to have it taken in. I thought things were useless, so I chose the size 11, red, floor-length gown. The fact that it was too small before alterations was bad enough. The way that it was altered was a nightmare.

The experienced alterations professional selected red material to add to the seams in my dress. What she didn't bother to do was to get a red piece that matched. When I tried it on, I realized that not only did I have a dress that Dolly Parton could wear, I couldn't lift my arms because it was two different colors. My mother paid the balance on the dress, we covered it in a plastic bag, and waited for the big night.

Our prom was held at a private country club. The committee and I had worked hard to make sure that all of the decorations were perfect, and that everything was in order. No matter how wonderful the room looked, I thought that everyone was looking at my unusual dress. I spent the entire night looking down at my cleavage, and hoping John wouldn't ask me to dance.

I thought that multi-colored dresses and proms were important in my life. The day my body began to fight back, "important" took on a new meaning.

Chapter 6
One Red Pill

Mother always gave me lunch money on Monday morning to last for the entire week. I would pick up Chandy on the way to school, and we would ride together. I drove a twelve-year-old, rusted out, farm pickup truck. All of my brothers had driven it before me, now it was my turn. Even though it was in bad shape, I was thankful to have something to drive. It was one of a kind, so whenever anyone spotted it, they knew that I was behind the wheel. This was one thing associated with me that I didn't feel self-conscious about. It became my trademark. Her name was "Little Blue."

Chandy and I were usually early to school. To kill time, we developed a bad habit of stopping at a local grocery store on the way. Chandy would get a biscuit in the deli, and I would use my lunch money for the week to purchase bags of candy. I would keep the candy in my locker, and snack on it between my classes. It usually didn't last a week, but I was out of lunch money, so I couldn't buy more until the next Monday.

I noticed that even though I wasn't eating meals, the candy intake was becoming obvious. I needed to do something to drop the weight. One Monday morning, instead of buying candy, I bought diet pills. The lady on the box looked fantastic. To make sure their effects would last, I bought twelve-hour, time-release capsules. I never did anything halfway.

I went into the bathroom in the band room before school and opened the box. I didn't bother to read the directions where I would have discovered that they weren't to be taken on an empty stomach. I put one red pill in the back of my throat and drank water directly from the tap. There, I was on my way to being skinny.

It didn't take me long to realize that I had made a huge mistake.

I became dizzy, nauseous, and disoriented. I had a hard time staying awake during class, and an even harder time walking down the hall. Every time I thought the pill was wearing off, the time-release formula would kick in. I have never had a cold medicine work like it said it would, why did this diet pill have to? I was too sick to eat at lunch, but thought I should try. I got a few bites down and gave up. I spent the rest of lunch with my head resting on the table.

That night we were going to an away football game with the band. I thought the bus ride would kill me. I sat up front and hung my head in the aisle the entire trip. When we stopped for supper, I sipped a diet soda. I couldn't believe that I felt so sick. It was the next morning before I really felt like myself again. I did the smart thing. I wrapped the package up in a paper towel, and threw them away at school. What I didn't do was ask for more money from my mom. I went the rest of the week without eating.

Mid-way through the year, I came down with the flu. I was sick for almost ten days. Even though I had become closely acquainted with the commode, I didn't like not being in control of when I threw up. I lost several pounds unintentionally. When my body recovered from the illness, my mind didn't.

I went back to school when I was physically well. Although the fever disappeared, the symptoms didn't. My parents became concerned because I was having trouble keeping any food or liquid down. Several people noticed that I had lost weight. Chandy looked me right in the face and said, "Don't you dare gain that weight back." I assured her that I wouldn't. I even got a few comments from some boys. Having a boyfriend didn't diminish the way I felt when other guys noticed me. After a week of continually throwing up, the doctor admitted me into the hospital. I was poked, x-rayed, weighed, and made to swallow horrible "potions" for tests. Everything that I ate was monitored along with everything that I threw up. I had several IV's to keep me from becoming dehydrated, and to get other nutrients in my body. After a week, the vomiting slowed down. Even though the doctors didn't have an explanation, they released me.

I had reached a point in my disease that I could regurgitate without help from my fingers or the end of a toothbrush. I could swallow air, forcing whatever was in my stomach to come back up. I was not proud of this, but it made purging much easier.

By now, I honestly wasn't sure if I was making myself sick, or if I was really physically ill. Whatever the cause, I liked the fact that I was losing more and more weight.

I began to quit telling my parents that I was still becoming sick after I ate anything. When they would ask, I would tell them that everything was fine. Lies were getting easier to tell. After my hospital visit, a friend put a half a dozen blueberry muffins in my locker. I munched on them in between each class. After school, I rid myself of each bite. I had, however, enjoyed them on the way down. I thought that I had mastered my disease. I was eating, I was purging, I was losing weight, and no one was worried.

While taking an algebra test late in the afternoon, I began to feel a burning sensation in my stomach. I had eaten nachos for lunch, purged them in the hall restroom, and continued on with my day as usual. I assumed that I had left some nachos in my stomach, and they were causing me the pain. As my stomach churned, a burning liquid would come up my esophagus and into my mouth. The taste was repulsive. I would swallow, and it would burn going back down. This continued until the amount in my mouth couldn't be contained. I rushed from my desk and threw open the bathroom door across the hall. As I lunged toward the commode, blood poured from my mouth. I had missed my mark and splattered blood all around. It was on the floor, running down the sides of the commode, and on the bathroom wall. Although I was horrified by the sight, I didn't have time to react. I continued to fill the commode with blood. With each flush of the toilet, I thought I could wash away my problem.

The stench from the brilliant red blood filled the stall. The horrible taste in my mouth was like nothing I had tasted before. I was no stranger to throwing up, but this was a whole new, horrifying experience. After I cleaned up the area, I stood in front of the mirror on the wall. The blood had splattered my face, and matted in my hair. How could I leave this bathroom looking like nothing was wrong? I tried the best that I could to make myself presentable. I washed my face and hair with drops of water, and went back to complete my test in silence.

I thought the nightmare was over. I tried desperately to concentrate on my test. Algebra was hard enough for me when I felt well; this was impossible. It wasn't long before the same taste and burning sensation reappeared. I tried to ignore it, but it was impossible. I waited as long as I could before I once again ran out of the room. The same bathroom, the same stall, more and more blood; my biggest concern was not the blood or my body. I didn't know how I could jump this hurdle without telling anyone that I had already fallen.

Chapter 7

"I'm Not Crazy!"

Caretaker, mediator, and overachiever are all words that are used to describe bulimics. Many who suffer tend to "mother" others without being able to identify their own needs first. With blood matted in my hair and splattered on my face, only one thought came to mind—*out of control.*

I was the president of my class. I was a good, conscientious student. I didn't smoke, curse, drink, or do drugs. I had been reared in a strong, nuclear family. What in the world was happening to me? I had no excuse to be in the shape that I was in. I felt completely hopeless.

Once again, I cleaned up the remainder of the blood from the inside of the stall, and on the outside of my body. I tried to compose myself as I returned to the classroom. I reluctantly told my teacher as little as I could about what had just happened. On the outside I seemed calm. Inside, I knew that I was dying. I was excused from completing the test. If one looks hard enough, some good can be found in every situation.

I had been working part-time at a local jewelry store. I enjoyed my job, but was concerned that I might lose it. The owner had been supportive when I was in the hospital the first time. He even brought me a large bouquet of colorful balloons. Although I thought he was pleased with my work, I knew that with or without me, things at the store had to be done. I called my employer before I called my parents. He told me not to worry, but to get well. I was relieved that he wasn't upset that I was going to be out for a few days.

When I called my mother at work, she wasn't there. I briefly described my situation to the secretary, and she told me I had a bleeding ulcer. She was trying to be helpful, but she wasn't. I had a thousand ideas about what was wrong with me. While I waited for my mother to pick me up, that number increased. I was immediately admitted to the hospital and the poking, charting, and x-rays all began again. For one test, I was sedated and a light on a tube was pushed down my esophagus and into my stomach. It was during this test that the doctor discovered that I had torn the lining of my esophagus. Hugh Downs was right.

The doctor returned me to my room while I was still groggy. As I lay on the hospital bed, I could hear the doctor talking with my mother. He told her that they had run many tests. This included a pregnancy test. At age sixteen, I was proud of my virginity. In fact, I had no desire to even have sex. I thought that this test was a complete waste of money. I don't think that my mother was too surprised when he told her that it was negative. He then mentioned that I was exhibiting some signs of the eating disorder, anorexia. However, he assured my mom that he didn't think that was my problem.

Groggy or not, I had heard enough. I mustered up enough strength to bolt up in bed and declare "I'm not crazy, I'm not pregnant, and I don't have anorexia!" My head hit the pillow as quickly as it had come off of it.

The doctor and my mother both ran to my bedside. They each began stroking my hands and insisting that I wasn't supposed to hear that conversation. They assumed that I was still sedated. They were a little too late. I had heard it, and I was angry with their speculations.

My official diagnosis was *Gastrorefluxive Esophogitus*. In layman's terms, it meant that I couldn't keep any liquid or solid down. I was also suffering from dehydration because of the constant vomiting. My potassium and sodium levels were low. I had really done a good job of messing things up this time.

I was fed a gourmet diet of clear broth and Jello. All of this I would eventually vomit into a bowl that the hospital had so kindly provided for me.

I had to have IV's inserted into my veins. Because of my dehydration, my veins were hard to locate. This meant being stuck several times. The nurses and I would joke that there were several flavors of IV's. I would order the milkshake and pizza flavors. Ironically, these were things that I never would have eaten and "kept."

During my first night in the hospital, I was monitored very closely. Throughout the night the nurses would check on me every two hours. Whenever they would come in, I would sit up in bed and try to have a conversation with them. After several visits long after midnight, one nurse told me that I didn't have to entertain her. She was simply doing her job, and I should try to sleep through it. Once again, I thought that I needed to smile and be cheerful for everyone. It was also another way to hide my fear. If I smiled, no one could see the terror in my eyes.

My mother started sneaking animal crackers into my room. I hadn't been able to keep anything down since my arrival, and they were a welcome sight. We thought we were being so tricky.

I liked the way they felt in my mouth. They had a sweet taste that was refreshing in comparison to clear broth and vomit. I never threw up one animal cracker that my mother fed me. I don't know if they made me feel like a little girl again, or if I was just desperate to eat something that I had to chew. To this day, I take animal crackers to friends who are sick, or just need a friendly boost.

The doctor asked a nutritionist to stop by my room and ask me some questions. She was interested in my eating habits. I told her that I ate three meals a day, and that I snacked on fruit and cheese. More and more lies. The sad thing was that even though she was a trained professional, she believed me. I didn't even think that I had tried to be convincing.

A family friend who was an employee at the hospital came by to see me. She talked to me for several minutes, and then she lifted my hand. She suggested that I might consider getting some professional help. I knew right away what she was referring to. She told me that I had nothing to be embarrassed about, but this could be a serious situation. I emphatically told her that I was "fine!" She left without a struggle, but I don't think that I convinced her.

I finally kept down enough animal crackers that the doctor released me. The tear in my esophagus had luckily healed without surgery. They had done all that they knew to do.

As I walked out of the hospital I held in my hand a prescription for Zantac. It was supposed to reduce my stomach acid so that I wouldn't throw up as much. In my heart, I held the pleasure that my jeans were three sizes to big.

Months later, I was having trouble with an ingrown toenail. I returned to the same doctor who had seen me at the hospital. As I sat inside the tiny room waiting for him to enter, I could hear him laughing. He was standing in the hall. "This is the girl," he said, "who couldn't quit throwing up. Her parents gave us thousands of dollars, and all of a sudden she got well." He continued to laugh. On that day he repaired my toe. Little did he know that he had crushed my spirit.

Chapter 8

When Does Obsession Begin?

Colorful flower beds, a beautiful creek, smelly trash cans, filthy kitchen sinks, moldy shower stalls, and green cow pastures all became my constant companions. I would throw up anything, anywhere. Sometimes when I needed to binge and purge, others were in the house. I had to plan my strategy carefully. Binging was not a problem. Our house was large, and people were usually scattered. I could easily take food into my room without anyone being aware of it. If someone was in my bathroom, I had to come up with an alternative plan.

During my senior year, I ran for class president. Before the election, I hung posters in the school to ask classmates for their votes. On my way to class one day, I noticed that something was written in pencil on one of my posters. As I got closer, I was able to read it clearly. Underneath where I had written, "Vote for Kate," were the words, "She's the one with the big boobs." I laughed it off and told my friends, "At least somebody noticed." Inside I was embarrassed and upset. It's not that I should win because I could do a good job, but because I was well endowed. With or without the help of the poster, I won the election.

Bulimia is often described as "the hidden disease." As far as my family knew, I had recovered fully from my mysterious illness. What they didn't know was that I was exhibiting many of the warning signs for my sickness.

I would repeatedly avoid eating meals with my family. I would claim that I was too busy or that I just wasn't hungry. Sometimes my parents would ask me to sit at the table so we could all be together, but they wouldn't force me to eat. I would watch as things were passed around the table. I would enjoy the smells of warm bread coming from the oven. I wanted to have this food in my mouth, but resisted with all that I had.

If I did enjoy a meal while I shared their company, I would immediately excuse myself. I would often turn the water or the radio on as I purged in the bathroom so that no one would suspect what I was doing. My muscles would react voluntarily, all I had to do was bend over. The only sound that could be heard was not my heaving, but the completely undigested pieces of the meal as they splashed into the commode. The force from the purging would cause my eyes to water and my mascara to smear. I was careful to wash away the mascara that was running down my face. Also, if the meal was colorful, stains would remain around the inside of the stool. Vomit would splash underneath the seat. All of this had to be cleaned completely in order for my tracks to be covered.

If the weather was pretty, I would sometimes go for walks at the end of a meal. It would always end up in the flowers, the pasture, or washing down the creek. I knew that no one would discover my regurgitated meals in these places.

Sometimes, my only option for purging was a sink or behind the shower curtain. I became masterful at pushing chunks of food through the tiny drain holes.

My last resort was the kitchen trash can. There my acidy vomit would fall between broken egg shells, torn envelopes, empty milk cartons, and day-old newspapers. The stench would fill the air, so I would take the trash outside. It appeared as if I was being helpful. The only one I was helping, or hurting, was myself.

My parents never noticed just how much food was disappearing. I'm sure they just assumed that three hungry, growing boys were consuming it. I was careful to always throw any wrappers in the trash cans. Some bulimics will hide them under chairs, mattresses, and pillows.

Another thing that my parents didn't observe was how obsessed I had become with weighing myself. I would always weigh the first thing in the morning. I had to use the bathroom and take all of my clothes off before I would step on the scale. I would also weigh before a binge so that I would know what I needed to weigh after a purge was completed.

Although bulimia is hard to detect, it doesn't diminish the lengths that sufferers will go to master it. To ensure that their stomachs are completely "cleaned out," I read that some consume large quantities of water. They regurgitate until the contents return crystal clear. A very small percentage even resort to sticking tubes into their stomachs to give themselves a stomach washout.

The warning signs that I exhibited were avoiding meals, visiting the restroom shortly after a meal, weighing frequently, and being obviously displeased about my figure. The fact that food was constantly disappearing was also a red flag. There are other warning signs that bulimics display. Some have dramatic fluctuations in their weight. Others stay up late at night so they can binge when everyone else has gone to bed. Some become isolated and disinterested in friends, work, or school. Depression is also something to be concerned about. Some warning signs are easy to recognize while others are impossible to detect. As a parent or friend, be aware of all unusual behavior. It may be the only cry for help you get.

It has always been important for me to be in control of every situation. As a Christian, I was reared to believe that without the ceremony of baptism, I was destined for eternal fires. I became baptized at an early age and took control over where I would spend eternity. At that time, I hadn't really accepted Christ into my heart, I just wanted to cover all of the bases.

As a student, I liked being in charge of things at school. Being the president of my class and a member of the student council, I felt like I had some control over decisions that were made concerning myself and my friends.

I knew that I was not pleased with my body from early on. As a young teenager, I did the only thing I knew how to do. I took control of what went into my body, and what came out of it. What I didn't know was that I wasn't in control because my eating disorder had taken complete control of me!

Chapter 9

Beyond the Smile

*J*ohn and I were sitting outside of the church building in his truck one Sunday night. We were trying to decide where we should eat supper. The conversation shifted, and I told him how generally displeased I was with my body. I told him that I wanted to be prettier, and look like anyone other than myself. I had become aware that he was taking the time to look at other females when they would walk past us. This fed my insecurities. I felt that if I was really what he wanted, he would only look at me. I realize now that I had unrealistic expectations for our relationship. John's response was, "I don't want a pretty girlfriend, I want you." Wow, what an answer.

Possibly if he had taken more time to think about what he was saying, his answer would have been different. He hadn't; so it wasn't. He started laughing and trying to explain what he meant. It didn't matter if he laughed or cried, I had heard what he said. My tiny self-esteem was pushed a little bit lower.

John and I had an on-again, off-again relationship. I had started dating him when I was fifteen. I was now a senior, and had no other significant boyfriends. If we broke up, I would allow myself a few weeks to see if anyone else would ask me out. They usually didn't, so John and I would get back together. One of my brothers tried to convince me that it would take a while for other guys to feel comfortable asking me out. He said that since I had been with John so long, guys wanted to make sure that I was finished with him. I don't know if others would have asked me out, but I was convinced that they wouldn't. I thought that it was better to be with someone that I wasn't always happy with than to be alone.

As my disease advanced, I began to binge while I was asleep.

40

I wasn't aware of these patterns until I woke up. I would get up in the middle of the night and raid the cabinets and the cookie jar. We always had something in our cookie jar. I would then climb back into bed and sleep until morning. Purging never occurred while I slept.

There were several ways that I discovered my habit. Sometimes I would wake up with food still in my mouth that I hadn't swallowed. Half-eaten cookies could be found on the table beside my bed. I could also feel crumbs in the sheets. My mouth would taste of sour milk or bitter orange juice.

Dental problems are common for bulimics. As the stomach acid washes over their teeth, it decays the layer of enamel. For some, nerve endings can become exposed and their teeth have to be crowned. I was concerned that a fat senior wouldn't look very glamorous with crowns on her teeth. My fears began to haunt my dreams.

I began to dream that every time I brushed, my teeth would crumble like sand. I feared that they would fall out when I opened my mouth to talk. I would scramble to explain my problem to my family and friends. When I awoke, I was relieved to discover that all of my teeth were intact. However, I was unaware of how much damage I was actually doing to them. I knew that the dentist would recognize that I had a problem when I went for check-ups. I quit going for my bi-annual visit. I thought that he might tell my family what he had observed.

At this point, my every waking thought was consumed with food and its effect on me. When my night eating and horrid dreams began, I knew that my every sleeping thought was consumed with food as well. I felt like I was spinning around in vicious circles. I knew that I was heading in the wrong direction, but I didn't know how to turn myself around.

Chandy came down with mono. She missed a lot of school and was assigned a homebound teacher. Since she was my constant sidekick, I felt lost without her. It was comforting to always have someone to walk to class with. It was nice to have someone to share details about weekend dates. We even shared all of our secrets. All but one.

I would call daily to check on her condition. Her mother would fill me in on how she felt. As the days passed, she began to tell me how thin Chandy was getting. More pressure. During one conversation she described how her arms had become so thin that she could get her whole hand around them. "She's nothing but bones," she'd say. I thought, "I've got to lose weight before Chandy gets well."

If I ate lunch at school, I would often get a salad. I would load it down with cheese, ham, and a gallon of salad dressing. One day, some very thin girls started laughing at another overweight student. I could hear them saying "How does she plan to lose weight with all of that salad on her plate. Why doesn't she just order a regular lunch. She's eating the same amount of calories." I evaluated what was on my plate. Even though they weren't talking about me today, they might tomorrow. From then on, if I ate salads, I barely covered the bottom of my plate. I assumed if they were thin, they must know what they're talking about.

If I ate a plate lunch, I would usually purge in the bathroom across the hall. Girls were everywhere. Some were reapplying make-up. Some were smoking. Some were doing what I was doing. No one ever said anything to me. Either they didn't notice, or they didn't care.

Then, I met someone who changed my heart and mind forever. I didn't realize what an incredible impact he would have on me. He was handsome, intelligent, emotionally secure, and a divorced teacher who was fourteen years older. The amazing thing about this man was that he immediately saw beyond my forced cheerfulness and into my heart.

Chapter Ten

Forbidden Fruit

*L*arry Watkins was certified to teach English, physical education, journalism, social values, health, and sociology. He didn't teach all of these subjects during the same year even though he was certified to do so. He also coached the girls' basketball team. The first thing that I noticed about Coach Watkins was not his ability as a teacher, or his broad smile. The first thing that I noticed was that he was ten years behind the fashion world. Kids at school called him the *Polyester King*. I knew that my wardrobe didn't compare to that of my friends, but I assumed that I was more up to date than he.

Chandy and I were taking a health course in his room. He was not the teacher for our class, so another teacher used his desk, supplies, and room. Our teacher happened to be the boys' basketball coach. Chandy and I sat in the front, very close to our teacher's desk. We were always concerned about our grades. We had discovered that we did better if we sat in the front of our classes.

Coach Watkins would forget things, and need to come into his class while we were in there. He would get things from his desk and discuss basketball plans with our teacher. He began to wander in and out frequently. Sometimes when I was supposed to be working quietly at my desk, I would talk to him. I enjoyed his sense of humor. At least, I knew he thought that he was funny. I started looking forward to health class in hopes that Coach Watkins would stop by. He usually did.

Exams were approaching quickly. Since Chandy and I were seniors with A averages, we convinced our teacher to let us write out the test. This is not the normal procedure in our public school system. However, we didn't have a normal teacher. He was a nice man, but

I'm not sure that teaching was his calling. We went into the gym where our health teacher's office was located. He had gotten us out of another class to gather information to begin working on the exam. We sat on the dusty floor outside his office while we went to work. It was obvious that mostly men were in charge of this area. It was filthy.

I noticed as we worked that Coach Watkins was resting on a couch in the hall. It was his planning time, and he was complaining of having a terrible headache. As Chandy and I worked, Coach and I talked. I don't know if we finished writing out the exam that day. I do know that I enjoyed the pleasant conversation that I had with the coach.

I began to intentionally leave things in my desk during health class so that I would have to go back and get them after school. It was the same concept as someone dropping their books to get attention. After a while, I didn't need an excuse to go by his room, I just did it. He would sit at his desk, and I would sit at a student desk. We always had something to talk about. Other students would wander in and out. They would talk for a few minutes and leave. I never was ready to leave. School was over at 2:45 P.M. Many days, I didn't walk out of his door until 5:00 P.M. The janitors came and left.

A rumor was circulated that he and I were dating "on the side." I would joke about it because I knew that people would believe what they wanted. I told Chandy the rumor. "I can understand why they're saying it," she said. That's what I liked, my best friend's honesty.

Afternoon visits weren't the only time we enjoyed each other's conversation. I knew that Coach got to school early. I was no longer picking up Chandy, so I started getting to school between 6:30 and 7:00 A.M. I knew it was unusual to want to spend so much time with a teacher, but he made me feel so comfortable. I felt like I could talk to him about almost anything. We didn't just talk. I helped him pick up the room, clean erasers, and put up bulletin boards. I had always dreamed of being a teacher and thought that I was getting some good experience. He enjoyed the help; I enjoyed the company.

Of course, meanwhile I was dating John. He was a talented carpenter and sometimes would use his talent to make furniture. He could take old, knobby boards and turn them into treasures. For Christmas that year, he made me an adorable child's wooden rocking chair. He had taken his time and used intricate equipment to make it extra special. It was priceless. It made me feel good to know that someone had spent so much time on something for me. As he sat under the tree in front of me, he smiled and said that it was for the children that we would one day have together.

Sitting in the chair was a large, brown, cuddly, teddy bear. If he was turned on, he played a variety of tunes. I assumed that he was for our future children as well. He won my heart instantly.

When I looked closely, I noticed a tiny package that was tied around his neck. It was wrapped in colorful Christmas paper. I had a feeling that it was something wonderful. As I opened it my hands were trembling. What I found was a sparkling opal and diamond ring. The opal was the large center stone, and a tiny diamond was on each side. I thought it was beautiful.

My parents always told me that diamonds should be given to me by important males in my life. They told me to not expect any from them. I was ready to turn seventeen, and I had gotten my first diamonds. It didn't matter to me that they were under a point each and that it takes one hundred points to equal a carat. They were still special, and I felt the same way.

Later on Christmas night, I sat on John's lap in his room. As he looked at the ring on my finger, he told me that it was a promise ring. That's the ring that one gets before one becomes officially engaged. This was a big step for me. I thought that it meant that I was off limits to anyone else. I had a promise ring, a steady boyfriend, and a promise for children in the future.

Some suspicious people think that opals are bad luck. I didn't heed the warning signs.

John found out that I was spending a lot of time in Coach's room. Needless to say, he wasn't pleased. He began to "surprise" me after school. He would wait for me in his truck. When I came out two hours after school was over, he would be upset. He didn't understand why I wanted to spend so much time with Coach. John warned me that he would try to put a move on me. There were a lot of things that I was unsure of at age seventeen. However, I was certain that Coach Watkins would never do anything to hurt me.

Later on, John began to come in the school and find me when it was time to go home. He didn't want his girlfriend to be spending so much time with another male. Even if the other male was a teacher who was fourteen years my senior.

Since I had turned fifteen, my goal in life had been to marry and have fourteen children. Even though I had dreams of being a teacher, I decided that college was out of the question. I assumed that I had found my companion for life. Remember, I had a promise ring. At that age, I thought rings meant destiny.

My parents tried to convince me that not going to college would be a tragedy. They had great hopes for my future. They were less than thrilled that I was considering settling down at a very early age. At college, I was concerned that I would be alone. I didn't want John to find someone else while I was gone. More importantly, he wanted me at home, because he was afraid that I might find someone else. I know now that if our relationship had been right, we could have been separated for years, and true love would have survived. We were both immature and insecure. I was selected once again by my classmates to receive the "wittiest" superlative award my senior year. The laughs just kept on coming.

During one conversation with Coach, he said something that changed everything. He looked me directly in the eyes, wiped the smile from his face, and said, "I know that you are always laughing on the outside and you seem so happy. I don't know what it is, but there is more to you than just a cheerful attitude. I think you are hiding a lot of distress and that you are hurting inside."

John was always concerned that I would leave and find someone else. Realistic or not, at that moment I knew that in my heart I already had left John emotionally.

The highlight of my day had been the time that I spent with Coach Watkins. I would arrive early in the morning and stay until the sun was on the way back down. Only once do I remember anyone in my family asking me why I was so late. Usually my mom was still at work and my Father and brothers were in the field. I'm sure that when asked, I made up a great excuse. No one asked again.

One night after my family had gone to bed, I felt a real need for conversation. I brought the portable phone into my room and dialed Coach's number. My heart was racing and my hands were trembling. A woman answered. "May I please speak to Larry Watkins," I said. Within seconds, he was on the line. "Don't guess you want to buy a newspaper." I wasn't selling newspapers, but I wanted him to know that it was me. I was trying to save him from being quick on his feet. I knew all that he had to say was, "I'm not interested." That wasn't exactly what I wanted to hear. In seconds, he was gone.

The next day, we talked about the call. We basically set up a schedule so that we knew when we could talk. I always had to call him. If our phone had rung at 11:00 P.M., my parents would have become very suspicious. The phone call became a nightly ritual.

I wasn't sure what I, a seventeen-year-old senior, had in common with a thirty-one-year-old teacher. I didn't know why I needed to spend so much time talking with him. I had a boyfriend. Obviously, there were many things that I couldn't talk to John about. I would save them for Coach. He always understood.

Although I enjoyed our talks, I felt like I was being sneaky. I didn't like feeling like I was going behind my parents' backs. My disease was still out of control. As I would lie in my bed and listen to his voice, I was never without food. I would hold the receiver up over my head and shove food into my mouth while he spoke. When it was my turn to respond, I would swallow and carry on the conversation. I didn't want him to hear me consuming entire cakes, bags of chips, and liters of diet drinks. When my stomach became so distended that it was uncomfortable for me to even move, I would think of an excuse to hang up.

The only light on at that time of night was a small night light in my bathroom. I didn't want to turn on the overhead light. It's brightness might be visible under doors. People had to think that I was asleep. In the darkness of my bathroom, I would purge the contents of my stomach. I would clean up my mess, splash my face, brush my teeth, and climb back into bed. I would then redial the phone. Coach had no idea what was going on.

Although I felt comfortable talking to Coach Watkins, I didn't tell him about my repulsive disease. I had heard him say once that he didn't understand people with eating disorders. "How can someone do something like that to their body," he had said. I could tell that he disapproved of the habit. I assumed that if he found out, he would disapprove of me. The thought of him turning away terrified me. Ironically, when I told him years later, not only did he support me, he held my hand all along the way.

I felt like my secrets were multiplying. I had struggled with my illness for four years. I had become masterful at hiding my symptoms. I knew that I was being deceptive. My parents thought that I was a good kid. What they didn't know scared me. On top of that, I felt differently about a teacher than I had ever felt about anyone. I knew I didn't think about John the way that I thought about Coach. It was obvious to me that if I could have chosen who to spend time with, I would have chosen Coach in a heartbeat. That was one more secret to add to my list. I was concerned that if my parents found out that Coach and I were talking so much they would be furious. Not only was I their daughter, I was their baby! They had a hard enough time dealing with the fact that John and I were together. They would freak if they found out about Coach. I had visions of them storming into the principal's office and demanding that he be reprimanded and replaced. Coach was careful to stay within his professional boundaries as much as he could. Although phone calls jumped over the line, he wasn't concerned. He didn't have to be, I worried enough for the both of us!

Chapter 11

Perfect Daddy

At age seven, I called my father "Perfect Daddy." I thought that he could do no wrong. When I would get home from school, Mom would say "Did you miss me?" "No, but I missed Perfect Daddy," I'd say. My mother would simply smile. She knew that my daddy and I had a special relationship.

At age seventeen, I called my father "stranger." We rarely spoke anymore. Most of our conversations turned into arguments where he would be angry, and I would be stubborn. He was desperate for me to go to college. He wasn't ready for his baby to have a serious boyfriend. If John and I would sit in the truck after an evening together, he would flick the porch light off and on. That was a signal for him to go home, and for me to come in. If John was inside, Dad would put on his pajamas. He would then come into the room where we were and tell us he was going to bed. He'd conclude by saying, "and Kate, it's time for you to go to bed too." Dad was struggling with his baby growing up. I was struggling too, but I was determined to go in the direction that my father opposed.

April 15, 1985, was a beautiful Sunday. My family and I all went together to church. I sat with John and his family. I enjoyed them. Especially his father. He was a Christian who was always kind to everyone, even me. He wasn't necessarily better than my father, just different. I liked his gentleness.

After church, lunch was served downstairs on this particular Sunday. We usually didn't stay for events after church, but on this afternoon, we chose to. When it was time to leave, I asked my mother if I could go home with John for the day. She agreed that it would be okay. I asked her to please not tell my father. I knew he would notice that I was missing when he got in the car, but I would be gone by then. I was trying to avoid a confrontation. Dad accused me of only going to church so that I could be with John. I denied it, but basically, he was right. I left that day without hugging, kissing, or even saying "good-bye" to my father. At that time, I didn't realize that it would be the last opportunity that I would ever have.

John and I went to Sunday night services together, and out for dinner. I arrived home at 10:00 P.M. That was my curfew on Sunday nights. I had to be alert on Monday morning for school. John usually walked me into the house. On this night, he let me out of the truck and headed back down the driveway.

In the darkness of the kitchen, I happened to notice a small note on the table. The house was unusually quiet. The writing on the note was sloppy and hard to read. Scribbled in pencil were the words, "took Dad to Williamson County Hospital." I put the note back on the table and casually walked out of the room. Then I realized that this was an important message. I read it again and my heart began to race. I bolted outside to see if John was still there. I was hoping that he could drive me to the hospital. He was gone. Even the dust from the long, gravel driveway had settled. I scrambled for my keys, jumped into "Little Blue," and sped toward the hospital.

I arrived through the emergency room entrance. I located my family immediately. My mother was pale but calm. She took my hand and assured me that everything was going to be okay. One of my brothers paced the tiled floor. All I knew was that my other two brothers were out of town and I was really afraid we would never be a whole family again.

Mom detailed how she and Dad had been dancing around the kitchen when he became limp and dizzy. "Honey," he said, "something's wrong." My mother helped him to the chair. He complained about his mouth being dry. When she returned with a glass of cool water, he couldn't raise his head. Mom knew he was having a heart attack. My brother had walked into the house at the same moment that Mom had had that realization. God sends angels just when one needs them.

My brother helped Mom put Dad's weakening body into the van. As Mom spoke to me about the incident, she knew Dad was sick. She thought that they had arrived on time. What Mom didn't know as the words flowed from her mouth was that Dad's blood was slowly ceasing to flow into his heart. He was having several more serious heart attacks behind the closed doors of the emergency room.

A tall man in a starched white coat walked into the waiting room. I noticed his jet black hair. He introduced himself as Dr. Jones. "Dr. Thomas is my husband's doctor," my mother said. With a harsh voice and quick words he echoed, "I'm his doctor now." My mother dropped her head and quietly said, "Okay."

He told us that my father's condition had worsened upon his arrival. He was aware that they didn't have sufficient equipment to treat him. He needed to be rushed to Nashville before things got any worse. We all agreed that we wanted the best for Dad.

My mother, brothers, and myself all followed the ambulance to Saint Thomas Hospital in Nashville. As I sat in the darkness of the van I prayed for my father's life. I pleaded to God for him to be okay. He was a young man of fifty-four. He was the father of four children. I was one of those children. He was also my mother's husband and companion of twenty-six years.

No one spoke during this endless ride. In my silence, I realized that I was wearing an opal necklace, opal earrings, and an opal promise ring. John had given them all to me. Could these shimmering, beautiful stones really bring bad luck? I was beginning to wonder.

I noticed the coolness in the spring night air as we ran into the emergency room. An older, balding gentleman came to us and spoke in a calming voice. He stood near my mother and suggested that she contact any out-of-town family members. "You're kidding," my mother said. "No Ma'am," he replied, "it is simply precautionary." My heart leaped. I watched as my poor mother scrambled for quarters. Why didn't they have a complementary phone for people who had loved ones that were dying?

After what seemed like hours, the doctor returned. As he spoke, he used words that were complicated and hard to understand. He graphically explained to us what wasn't working, but he never told us specifically what was wrong. I was young and intimidated by his age and wisdom. However, his mumbo jumbo was beginning to irritate me. I looked him right in the face and said, "So, in other words, you have absolutely no idea what is wrong with my father." He reluctantly agreed that I was correct.

My father was moved from the emergency room into the critical care unit. Visitation was short and only during scheduled times. No one told us the rules, and we didn't bother to read any signs. We wandered aimlessly into the ward trying desperately to locate my father. Once we were discovered, we were quickly exited through the large, steel doors. For hours we waited. These were the final hours of my father's life, and we were spending them waiting for permission to be with him. Finally a nurse approached us and said, "Isn't anyone going to visit Mr. Sullivan?" By the tone in her voice, I felt that she was implying that we didn't care about him. She was wrong.

I walked slowly toward my father's room while holding my mother's hand. The sight of my sick father's body was hidden by tubes and machines. Things were pumping, clicking, and dripping around my daddy. One cylinder was filling up with blood. "Where is that blood coming from?" I asked the nurse. "We don't know but we are trying to keep it out of his lungs," she replied.

Only hours before, I had heard my father laugh. I had seen the sparkle in his eyes. I had watched him kiss my mother. This was the man who had taught me to ride horses, yet, he always insisted on saddling them because I might not get it on tight enough. The man who dug up the backyard after I flushed ten maxi pads down the commode while insisting that it wasn't my fault. The man who actually nailed the windows in our home shut when James Earl Ray escaped and I was sure he was heading straight towards us. The man who was the appreciative recipient of homemade lemonade that I brought to him in the summer's heat. The man who always made me say "Good-bye" when I left the house. This was my *Perfect Daddy*.

I lifted his large, strong, cold hand off of the sheets. "Daddy," I said in a child-like voice, "the angels are in here." I got no wink, no smile, no response. My mother asked about his kidneys. The nurse's information was not comforting. "They are beginning to fail," she said. I gave him a small kiss on his bald head and left the room.

A few hours later, they rolled him past my family on a stretcher. I didn't stand up to look at him as he passed. I could see a body but not my father. They were going to try and install a pacemaker. He was in the operating room for less than an hour.

As the doctors walked toward us, we knew the news was bad. They led us into a private room off of the hall. I sat at my mother's feet. The doctors told us that my father's heart had basically exploded. He died early in the operation, and never really had a chance.

I tried to comfort my mother by saying "He's with God at this very moment." My mouth was saying one thing while my heart was thinking, "My gosh, I've killed my father."

Chapter 12

All My Fault

On April 15, 1985, as I sat at my mother's feet, I wept huge tears. I knew that Daddy's death was my fault. I had to shut my heart off. No more thoughts of Coach could enter my mind. He came to visit me at the funeral home. As we spoke, I clung to John. I was cold and to the point. I was rude. He left as quickly as he had arrived. He didn't even sign the registry.

He called me after I got home. When I realized that it was him on the line, I panicked. My mother had answered the call. She thought nothing of it. When he asked me in his sympathetic voice how I was, I responded quickly. "I'm fine, thanks for calling. Bye." Click.

I was determined to get him out of my system. It didn't matter that I needed him more now than I ever had. It didn't matter that simply his presence would have been so much more comforting than any words or affection from John.

I knew that God was punishing me. If I had been a good daughter, I could have spared my family this pain and grief. If I didn't have secrets, my Daddy would still be here. God had given me a message to "shape up." I was planning to heed his warning.

Coach Larry Watkins lost his father to a stroke when he was sixteen. Coach was a star basketball player. His father had made arrangements to watch him play that night. He had never seen any of his games before. His father didn't make it to the game. He suffered a severe stroke, and was dead in several days. Until now I had been sympathetic, but now all I knew was that my daddy was dead within thirteen hours after his first attack and I felt responsible. Our stories had a lot in common, but I was determined that we would never compare notes. My guilt stood in the way of any possible happiness.

What Is a Father?

A father is a creature that is forced to endure childbirth without an anesthetic. A father growls when he feels good and laughs loud when scared half to death.

A father never feels worthy of the worship in a child's eyes. He's never quite the hero his daughter thinks; never quite the man his son believes him to be, and this worries him— sometimes. So he works hard to try to smooth the rough places in the road for those of his own who will follow him.

A father gets angry when the school grades aren't as good as he thinks they should be. So he scolds his son—though he knows it's the teacher's fault. A father gives his daughter away to another man who is not nearly good enough so he can have grandchildren who are smarter than anybody's. A father makes bets with insurance companies about who will live the longest. One day, he loses and the bet is paid off to those he leaves behind.

I don't know where a father goes when he dies but I have an idea that after a good rest, wherever it is, he won't just sit on a cloud and wait for the girl he loved and the children she bore. He'll be busy there, too—repairing the stairs, oiling the gates, improving the streets—smoothing the way.

—Anonymous

My father wasn't perfect. No one is. I took to heart many of the things that he said to me during the seventeen years that we were together. He wasn't responsible for my eating disorder. Many years of low self-esteem, innocent teasing by brothers, and an unreasonable goal set by myself were all contributing factors. Two people can be told the same thing and they will process it differently. If I was told that something looked good on me, it meant that what I wore yesterday didn't. If I was asked to bring dessert to a party, it meant that since I was fat I must bake a lot of sweets. When it came to how I thought about myself, the glass was always half empty.

As my family and I gathered around my father's closed coffin, we all held hands and I prayed. I thanked God that we had gotten to be a part of Daddy's life. I was thankful that he had taught us to be responsible and hard-working. I was thankful that up to this point, our family hadn't been separated by death or divorce.

As the warm tears ran down my cheeks and the words came from my heart, John looked on in disapproval. He believed that a female was forbidden to pray in the presence of a male. I was certain that God had heard my words; I didn't understand why John had tried to diminish them. Once again, I felt misunderstood.

I returned to school the day after my father's precious body had been returned to the dust. My friends weren't sure what to say. I tried to make it easy for them. The smile on my face was as broad as ever. I was determined to make it through this trauma, and I wouldn't inconvenience anyone in the process.

Chapter 13

Wedding Bells and Good-bye

The following words were written in a sympathy card for my family. The sender had recently experienced a loss and the same poem was written to her. She thought they would help comfort my family. The words could make me feel warm, but they ultimately didn't keep me from the cold.

> As good friends walk beside us,
> On trails that we must keep,
> Our burdens seem less heavy,
> And the hills are not so steep.
>
> The weary miles pass swiftly
> When taken in joyous stride,
> And all the world seems brighter
> When friends walk by our side.

Coach Watkins and I only spoke when we passed in the hall. I no longer arrived at school early and left late. I got there just in time for class to start and left when the last bell sounded. I seemed just like all of the other students. It wasn't easy. Sometimes I would go out of my way to walk by his classroom, but only when I knew he was teaching. I didn't want us to be able to talk. I was trying desperately to convince myself that he was no more than a teacher.

I was concerned about my mother. She had her children, she had a good job, and she had the support of friends. What she didn't have was a husband.

As my senior year was coming to a close, I had definitely decided not to go to college. My only other option was to get engaged. John and I happened upon a small jewelry store that was advertising a huge sale. I thought that if I was ready, the time to buy a diamond was when they were on sale. I convinced myself that I was ready.

One afternoon, we visited the store. We located a wedding ring set that I thought he could afford. It wasn't very pretty, but I thought that didn't matter. If I really loved him I would settle for something less than what I wanted. What I didn't know at the time was not only was I settling for a ring, I was also settling for my lifetime partner.

I waited in the truck while John's credit was checked. We both knew that there wouldn't be any problem. As he walked toward the truck, I didn't notice a bag. "Maybe," I thought, "they wouldn't let him charge it." For a second I was relieved. When he pulled a velvet box from his pocket, I tried to be happy. "Do you want to do this now?" he said. "Sure." "Okay," said John, "will you marry me?" That was it? Where were the trumpets, the firecrackers, the balloons? I slipped it on my finger. "Yes," I said. There, we had done it. We were engaged. It wasn't exciting and I didn't feel thrilled. However, on the outside, I sure was smiling. As we drove toward my house, I secretly thought, "What in the world have you just done?!"

The jewelry store was only twenty minutes from home. For the entire twenty minutes, I worried about what my mother might say. Dad had only been dead for about a month. Now, I was going to shock her again.

When we got there, we found her inside. Her clothes were dirty and her face was tear-stained. I ignored what I saw and blurted out the "good news." She didn't hug me, cheer, or even smile. Even though I didn't feel pleased, it would have been nice if she could have faked it like I was. Guess God didn't make mothers to be dishonest.

I realized that she had been cleaning out my father's closet. Years of flannel shirts, faded jeans, and cowboy boots were going to be sold at a charity store. It seemed less than a fitting end for my dad. I felt terrible because I had overlooked her pain. I felt even worse because selfishly I was upset that she wasn't celebrating with me. John didn't understand why Mom wasn't happy. I did, for several reasons.

Over the weekend, I decided that I just didn't like the way the ring looked. Love or not, if I was going to have it on my hand for a lifetime, I wanted to like it. I thought the appearance of the setting was making me have second thoughts. What was really happening was that I was coming to my senses and I needed an excuse to return it.

I hid the ring in my purse on Monday morning and returned it after school. I had shown it to Chandy during the day and she wasn't impressed either. John was less than pleased that I decided to return it. I convinced him that he wasn't the problem. I was getting good at acting.

I was seventeen and thought that if I didn't marry John, I would die an old maid. What I didn't realize then is that God fills one's life with potential mates. I just assumed that I was too ugly for anyone else to love me. I thought that unsure and unhappy was better than all alone.

A few weeks later, a close friend convinced me to room with her at a Christian university. The campus was only thirty minutes from home. I decided that I would try it for a little while. John wasn't thrilled with my decision, but I told him that we would be okay. I sent off my application and was easily accepted.

The day that I graduated from high school, I gave Coach a small box. It was wrapped in white paper and tied with a blue ribbon. Inside was the friend's poem that had been written to comfort my family. I had charted out a pattern and cross stitched it myself. I had yearned for his company with each stitch. Not speaking to someone doesn't erase them from your heart. The gift was my form of closure. I would graduate, leave Franklin High School, and drop my memories of Coach Watkins at the door, I thought.

Chapter 14

Make a Wish

My high school friend and college roommate, Laura, and I had a good time shopping for things to put in our dorm room. We felt like we were a step closer to adulthood. However, we knew that we were far enough away that we could still act like kids. I was able to make financial decisions concerning purchases, yet my mom was still responsible for writing the checks. It was a no-lose situation. I had no idea at the time how great I had it.

As I walked onto the beautiful campus for the first time, I immediately felt out of place. The first things that I noticed were not the monstrous buildings, the towering trees, or the infamous Bison mascot. The first thing that I noticed was that every female seemed to be more prim and proper than myself. They were all beautiful. Their outfits were a part of the latest fashions and their figures seemed perfectly sculpted. Of course, everyone didn't fit this stereotype, but I didn't seem to notice them.

I looked down at my jeans, old sweater, and dirty tennis shoes. Had I made a poor decision? I realized that it was too late, so I resorted to what I knew best, laughter and control. After Laura and I were settled in our room, I began to help the other girls in my suite unpack. I bounced around from room to room, introducing myself and making everyone else feel at home. We all laughed and shared interior decorating tips for our tiny cubicles. After several hours, one girl said, "What's your major?"

"What?" I said.

"Aren't you a senior?" she asked.

"No, this is my first day."

She was flabbergasted. She assumed that because I was seemingly comfortable, the university had given me the job of getting new students settled in. Wow, I must have been convincing. She hadn't even noticed my old jeans. I had once again fooled others into thinking that I was funny and in control.

As I met new friends, I loved the company but always compared them to myself. One of my closest friends was a fashion model. I admired Kathy because the beauty from her smile had a straight line to her heart. She had a sweet spirit that I gravitated to. Her fragile, gentle voice was quite the opposite of my loud, overpowering one. Once again, I had found someone else that I wanted to be like.

During my first semester at the university, I was a regular at mealtime. That is, if I was by myself. Breakfast consisted of bowls of Captain Crunch cereal and assorted pastries. Lunch was whatever they were serving plus two large chocolate chip cookies with ice cream sandwiched in between. Supper was just a lot of everything.

If I ate with friends, I ate what they ate. If they had a salad and fruit, I had a salad and fruit. If they only drank tea, I sipped on a glass of tea.

Between classes, I scavenged for loose change to put in the vending machines. I would search under cushions, outside in the dirt, and around the parking lot. I was desperate to binge because I needed to purge. At home, food was always available to me and it was free! If I ate at the university, I had to pay for it. Only three meals a day were included in my tuition. Normally, that is how often people eat. I was far from normal. I was struggling to keep my disease alive. I needed to have some relief from my insecurities.

Planning a purge in a public restroom was not always easy. Someone was always in the suite because everyone had different class schedules. I learned to become more manipulative.

Our restroom was usually nasty. We were supposedly sharing the cleaning responsibilities, but it wasn't working well. Before a purge, I would often find bloody tampons that hadn't been flushed floating in the stool. Mold crept between the tiles on the wall. The scent was a mixture of expensive perfumes and cheap hairspray. No matter what the smell or the obstacle, I would hold back my hair, close my eyes, and complete the disgusting ritual. I was putting my face where strangers put their excrement.

Despite my constant binging and purging, I still gained several pounds. The chocolate chip cookies with ice cream weren't helping. The extra pounds lowered my self esteem while increasing the numbers on the scale. When I would stand on the scale in the morning, I would emotionally torture myself as I saw the numbers going up. I would beat myself in the legs, and frantically shift the scale on the floor. I would weigh on the tile and then on the carpet. I was desperate for the numbers to decrease. I thought that they held the key to my self-worth. If they were low, I was okay. As they rose, my worth decreased.

I would stand completely naked in the cold dorm room. Not even the tiny rubber band in my hair could remain. If the numbers didn't please me, I would go hours without eating or drinking anything. Then I would weigh again, naked, and see if my suffering and done any good. I was so fixated on my weight that it was hard to concentrate on my studies.

Several weeks into my first semester, the doctors discovered that John's father had a brain tumor. I thought that it was more important for me to be with John than at school. I would attend my classes then leave as quickly as I could. Many nights I slept at their home and returned for class in the morning. I didn't spend much time on homework or studying for tests. My mind was focused on many other things. I decided to quit school and join the world of the working.

Though stress and sadness were prevalent, John and I became officially engaged, again. We drove to a beautiful fountain that was in front of an enormous office building in the city. I had always loved elaborate fountains. John would have extra pennies with him at all times in case we happened upon a fountain. I would hold the penny tightly, make a wish, and watch it break the surface of the water and settle to the bottom. John thought that this fountain would be the perfect place to ask me to be his wife.

As we opened the truck doors, it began to rain. The fountain was turned off and was simply a still mass of water. The beautiful setting turned wet and flat. He placed the ring on my finger as I wiped the drops of rain from my face. Why did everything that was intended to be wonderful with us, get messed up. Once again, I ignored the warning signs.

Our decision came only days before John's father passed away. His father had graciously given us his approval.

I convinced myself that I was happy about our upcoming wedding. With the death of our fathers, we were pulled closer together. We were determined that since our children couldn't enjoy them, we would share their fine qualities with them. We talked about many things as we discussed our future. One thing that I failed to mention was the disease that was slowly killing me.

Chapter 15

Shattered Reflections

I applied for a job at a local dry cleaners. I realized that without a college education, my opportunities were limited. However, I could have set my sights a little higher. I would make five dollars an hour if I got the job. There were no benefits. I had no idea what it took to make a home and a family run. To my mother's credit, she was pleased when I was hired. Although it wasn't her dream for me, she made me feel that it was okay to work at a cleaners. She never once belittled me. I did appreciate her for that.

Along with asking, "Would you like light, medium, or heavy starch, Sir?" I was busily making wedding plans. As I ordered flowers, selected china, and celebrated with friends, my head was spinning. I couldn't discern between second thoughts and the normal jitters.

My mother and I shopped for a wedding gown at the same store where I had purchased my multi-colored prom dress. Some people never learn. I selected the very first dress that I tried on.

John was working several blocks down from the store on the day that I made my decision. As I skipped down the street to see him, I thought about how excited he would be to hear that I had chosen my perfect gown. When I walked in the building, he was sitting in a room with several of his friends. Immediately when I saw him I shared my excitement. I expected him to pick me up and swing me around like in the movies. Well, if he couldn't swing me, he could at least act like he was happy. The only expression that he sent my way was a blushing face, and a small snicker. I knew right away that I had embarrassed him in front of his buddies. I was confused.

Not only was John not excited about my dress, he didn't get excited about much of anything. Our personalities were completely opposite. That didn't mean that mine was better than his, it simply meant that we weren't at all alike. I selected the flowers, the china, the crystal, and the invitations. It bothered me that we were planning to be one, and we couldn't even make decisions together.

As the special day approached, I begin to think about "what if's." What if Daddy hadn't died? What if I had stayed in college? What if Coach Watkins had kept in touch after high school? What if I invited him to the wedding. I did consider it, but I knew that it would cause a confrontation with John. What if I was pleased with myself and wasn't afraid of being alone?

I always thought that it was important for husbands and wives to share everything. I knew that secrets could tear a marriage apart. I knew that I held a huge secret in my heart, and thought I needed to share it with my future partner. John was unaware that I threw up after each date. He didn't know that I hid food in my room and ate while I was actually asleep. He didn't know that I longed to be anyone other than who I was.

I stored up my energy and told him about my repulsive disease. I left out many details because I didn't want him to be disgusted with me. After several minutes of explaining, I paused for a response. He slowly lifted his hand, patted me on the head, and said, "We'll pray about it."

I realized that I had told him something that was hard to understand. I knew that I was explaining behavior to him that was not normal. I knew that it was scary. What I didn't know was that he would take it so lightly. I'm not diminishing the power of prayer. However, I had been praying about this monster inside of me for six years. Every night I would lie in bed and beg God to let me be okay. I wanted to be able to eat normally and let food actually digest. I was praying; I needed more. I needed him to comfort me. I needed him to tell me that he was going to find me some help. I needed him to do anything other than pat me on the head like a puppy. I already felt like a dog; I guess that was an appropriate response! John never mentioned it again.

Only twice in six years had I told anyone my horrific secret. They were both people that I trusted. Chandy jokingly suggested that I was crazy. John completely dismissed my fears. It would be years before I could trust again.

On May 24, 1986, the heavens opened up. It was the day of my wedding and I received major signals from above. There weren't showers of sunbeams, but torrential rains, hail, and a nearby tornado. It has been said that the number of raindrops that fall on one's wedding day will be the number of tears that are shed during the marriage. I had opals, death, and tornadoes against me. I needed lightning to strike me as well.

With twelve bridesmaids and twelve groomsmen in the wedding party, the church was bustling with excitement. We were getting married in the church where we had been reared, baptized, met, and fallen in love. We had received pre-marital counseling from the minister who was performing the ceremony. We had a storybook beginning.

In the bridal room two hours before the ceremony, I discovered that once again my dress was not right. It had been delivered to the church a few hours earlier. I hadn't had time to try it on. Extra material was to have been sewn in so that my bra would not be visible. The alterations professional had not sewn in enough. One could see the lace on my bra better than the lace on my dress. There wasn't time to send it back. Pictures were to be taken in thirty minutes.

Someone came up with the brilliant idea that I go braless. Braless, braless, yes, they said braless. I was nineteen years old and had never gone braless a day in my life. Not many people with a FF cup do. I had no choice. I removed my bra.

Everyone stood around and watched while I observed my braless profile. The beautiful silk was gathering around my breasts and my nipples could be observed around the vicinity of my bellybutton. I thought I looked appalling, but knew I had no other options.

The music was playing beautifully. The candles were all sparkling in the dimly lit auditorium. My dearest friends were positioned in front of the flowered alter. I was holding my grandfather's arm. Months of planning and thousands of my mother's dollars had made this day a reality. As I slowly walked down the carpeted aisle, the only thing I thought about were my two jiggling bosoms. A seven-hundred-dollar dress and wiggling breasts. As I reflect on that memorable event, it seems only justice that the alterations professional and the wedding gown store are no longer in business. They caused me such misery that there must have been other unhappy customers like me. The ceremony was completed. Presents were displayed and cake was cut. Hugs were shared and rice was thrown. We drove off into the night towards bliss.

Chapter 16

Breakfast Is Served

When a couple gets married, each partner has certain expectations for the future relationship. My parents had been fortunate to have a strong marriage. As I got older, I was able to recognize aspects of their union that I liked and ones that I didn't.

I liked that my mother and father were openly affectionate in front of their children. It gave us security during a time that many marriages were beginning to fail. I thought it was special that they sat alone in the car after we returned from church. They would sit in the driveway for up to two hours. They needed quiet time together, and this was where they enjoyed it. I liked that Dad usually complimented Mom after supper was over. It was obvious that her hard work was enjoyed and appreciated.

The main thing that bothered me about their marriage was the way that they handled fights. They didn't argue often, but the tension in the house could be felt by all when they did. My mother could actually go a week without speaking to my father. Dad liked to just forget about things that he might have done to hurt Mom's feelings. He tried to joke his way out of a lot of things as well. Mom liked official apologies. Somehow, they usually ended up meeting in the middle and working things out. Dad never spoke ugly words to my mother and his fist was never raised.

I know that my groom must have had certain expectations about our life together as well. I feel sure that I let him down many times. We thought that "love" was all we needed. We never took the time to talk about the important things like who was going to take out the garbage and fold the clothes. Getting married is the easy part; staying married is an entirely different thing.

We honeymooned in the beautiful small town of Gatlinburg, Tennessee. We had been there before with his family, but this time we were all alone. As we drove through the colorful mountains, we couldn't believe that we were husband and wife. I was nineteen and John was twenty-two. The day before, we had vowed before our friends, our family, and our God that we would be together forever.

We visited many trendy shops while we toured the town. We had a good time selecting things for our new home. We also spent a lot of time eating. I had not been eating on a regular basis before the wedding. I had lost some weight and was still concerned about my appearance. I wanted to be smaller, but didn't want to mess up our special time together. I decided to resist binging and purging while we were honeymooning.

In John's house, food had been just as important as it had been in mine. That was one thing that we did have in common. We honeymooned for five days, ate our weight in fat grams, and returned home to our new condo ten pounds heavier.

When one confuses their system by binging and purging, it's hard for the body to process food that is not purged. I had been throwing up most of what I had been eating for at least the last year. When I kept every meal I ate for five days in a row, my body decided to store it all. It didn't know when it might see this much food again.

My job at the cleaners began at 7:00 A.M. I thought that a good wife always made her loving husband a hearty breakfast. For several days after we returned from our honeymoon, I would get up at 4:00 A.M. I would prepare homemade biscuits, fried eggs, tenderloin, fresh fruit and orange juice. John didn't like pulp in his juice so I would sometimes strain it. I would gently wake John up at 5:00 A.M. and proclaim, "Breakfast is served."

I watched John slowly lift his tired body out of bed. I sat beside him at the table while he struggled to keep his head up and his eyes open. After his last bite, he would crawl back to bed and continue sleeping. One afternoon he said to me in a gentle voice, "I appreciate what you're doing, but could you please let me sleep in the morning? I can fix myself something after I get up." John ate cold cereal from the next morning on. I thought good food meant good marriage. I was trying to do my part to get the ball rolling smoothly. I still continued to get up at 4:00 A.M. I used the time that I had been cooking to exercise.

My routine began with only several sit ups and a few push-ups. I was desperate to work off what I had gained on my honeymoon. I remembered an exercise bicycle that my father had purchased a few years before his death. He had ridden it twice. His intentions were good but his body was lazy. I got permission from Mom and brought it home.

Exercising became something that I looked forward to. It was also something that I became very obsessive about. I didn't know at the time that other bulimics used exercise to purge. I thought that I had happened upon something new. I could purge and exercise. Surely I could lose weight that way.

A friend at work introduced me to a new diet. It was called the Hilton Head Metabolism Diet. One was supposed to exercise twenty minutes after two microscopic meals a day. I purchased the book and followed the program completely.

I decided that if I continued to get up at 4:00 A.M., I wouldn't be able to eat, wait twenty minutes and then exercise. I was determined to make this diet work. I quit binging and purging and used this book as my guide to happiness. I set my alarm for 3:00 A.M. I would get up, eat one piece of dried toast and a half of a grapefruit. I would then wait for twenty minutes. I'd hop on my bike and pedal like crazy for thirty minutes. I would then get ready for work.

As I began to see results I became terrified that I might sleep through an exercise schedule. I thought that if I missed one turn on my bike, all of my hard work would be in vain. I started getting up at 1:00 A.M. I would eat my "breakfast," ride, then go back to sleep for two hours. Even though my body was exhausted, it wasn't always easy to go back to sleep. My heart was racing, my hair was sweaty, and my body was smelly. John never moved when I got out of bed or when I go back in.

I was working diligently on my diet but not on my marriage. When John would get home from work my main concern was eating so that I could exercise. I didn't spend time with him at the table to talk. I ate, cleaned up, then it was time to exercise. I was exhausted because of the small amount of food that I was eating, the fact that I was up at 1:00 A.M., and the rate at which I exercised.

I not only became more and more obsessed, but I also became anti-social and rude. If couples would invite us out for supper I would panic. I wouldn't be able to order my required meal, and I wouldn't be able to exercise on time. I knew that it would all go to my hips. If John's mother, who was an excellent cook, invited us over, I would take my own paper bag. As his family ate wonderful things that were baked, fried, and creamed, I would force down a boiled egg and dry piece of bread. His family would get upset with me. I didn't understand why they wanted me to be fat. I thought that they were all in a conspiracy to make me gain weight. Although I wasn't binging, my mind, my actions, and my body were out of control.

Many people noticed that I lost twenty pounds in a month. One lady even suggested to my mother that I looked anorexic. Normally people gain weight when they marry. My excuse for losing weight after our marriage was that "we were to poor to afford food." What a lie. People would laugh, but they had no idea what a struggle I was going through. I wasn't sleeping. I wasn't eating. I was exercising away any fat that remained. Sadly, I didn't see that I was sacrificing my relationship to have "the perfect body." I believed that I was doing it for my new husband. I thought that he wanted me to look different. At times, he had commented about other women. He had told me what he would change about me if he could. I was trying to be a perfect wife for him. I had no idea how completely misguided my thinking was.

Chapter 17

Comfortable Routines

ecause of my rigorous diet plan, I reached a weight that I felt comfortable with. Not only had I lost pounds, but I had lost inches as well. I went off of the diet, yet wanted to maintain my weight loss. For a month I had followed word for word the advice of a diet book. I had learned nothing about nutrition or maintenance. I was not interested in being healthy but in being thin. I was terrified that within days I would be "fat" again. I forgot about maintaining. I returned to eating anything that I wanted and purging everything that I ate. The cycle had started once again.

Since our wedding I had been taking oral contraceptives. I took them before I ate, I knew that they would come back up with the undigested meal. If I become careless, I would become pregnant. Now I had to worry about maintaining my secret and manipulating my birth control.

After my diet, my purging was worse than it had ever been. I was miserable both physically and mentally. I would use my lunch time to sleep in a chair. If I ate at work, I ate cottage cheese and fruit. Once again, I decided to trust someone with my secret.

The lady at work that had introduced me to my diet had become a close friend. I told her about my struggle. When she heard my story, she immediately told me where I could get some help. I felt relieved. She didn't laugh, she didn't ignore me, she was honestly concerned. The clinic that she spoke of was in Nashville. She even told me that if insurance wouldn't cover my sessions, they would charge according to my income. I drove home that day with some hope in my heart.

I made an appointment to speak with a counselor. John agreed to go with me. I lied and told the center that I had no medical insurance.

69

I didn't want my illness to be written down anywhere. It was too risky that someone else might find out.

I spent an hour in a small cubicle with a counselor. I tried to remain cheerful and answer the questions in the way that I thought I was supposed to. I didn't lie, I simply didn't tell the entire story. Although my heart was ready to be healed, my mind didn't know how to start the process. My entire life I had everyone thinking that I was in control. It was hard for me to give that persona up for a stranger.

During one point of the session I asked, "Do I have something wrong with me? I mean do I really have an eating disorder?" What a ridiculous question. I was binging and purging, overexercising, hiding food, eating in my sleep, and weighing myself obsessively. Did I think that was normal? For me . . . it was.

The counselor confirmed my fears. She told me that when people struggle with food, it is considered an eating disorder. "Struggle" seemed to be too small a word to describe what I was going through.

When my session was over, I exited into the waiting area. That was when I noticed John. He was sitting on the couch with the paper held up high. It was concealing his face. He might have been reading an article at the bottom of the page, but I assumed that he was trying desperately not to be noticed. I felt embarrassed and ashamed. If I was a good wife, I thought, he wouldn't have to be dealing with this situation.

Periodically during the week, we talked about me returning to the clinic. We never talked about my initial session. John kept expressing a concern for the financial aspect of my recovery. Basically, I felt like I wasn't worth eighty dollars a month. It was a lot of money for a young married couple to spend on something as frivolous as "recovery." After all, we could use that money to buy a new couch. Then, when I was too weak to stand, at least I would have a nice place to rest my sickly body. I got the message loud and clear.

The clinic sent me a letter expressing their concern because I had not returned. In big, bold letters I wrote, "I'm well" across the top of the page. I sent the letter back, and never heard from them again. I'm sure they realized that I wasn't ready to recover. Even if I had been, I knew I couldn't do it without support. I had none.

I got a new job three months later. A very dear teacher of mine was becoming the principal at a new elementary school. He thought that I needed to be doing something other than hanging up other people's dirty clothes. He hired me to be a library assistant. Since I had always wanted to be a teacher, I instantly adored my new position. I decided to return to school at night and pursue my teaching degree.

I was working for eight hours, and spending the rest of the time studying, throwing up, and exercising. I would snack on pretzels at school and begin to binge immediately when I walked into our home. I was ravenous. I would binge and purge until John came home. I would then cook supper, eat, purge, and exercise. If I had a night course, I would exercise when I got home. Sometimes that was 10:00 P.M. Time that I should have spent with John was spent focusing on myself and my disease.

Not only was I riding my exercise bike, but I was following work-out videos as well. I was also taking a physical education course for college credit. My heart rate was becoming erratic. I noticed that I was having trouble keeping my mind focused and completing thoughts. I was starving my body and abusing my brain. At work I would be as cheerful as I could possibly be. At home I was a tyrant.

One afternoon, I saw a commercial for a 1-800 phone number for people with eating disorders. If a call didn't cost me twenty dollars, maybe it was worth a try. A woman with a soft voice answered the phone. "I have been bulimic for eight years," I said quietly. "Is there anything that you can tell me over the phone to make me better?" The kind volunteer began to tell me that there were numerous facilities where I could receive help. "No," I interrupted, "can you just tell me over the phone something to make me well?" "Not over the phone," she said. "Thank you anyway," I responded. I had run into another wall. I wanted so desperately to be well. However, it couldn't take time, money, and no one could know about it.

Chapter 18

The Rush to Replenish

Going grocery shopping was a race against the clock. I would fill my basket with boxes of cookies, numerous frozen pizzas, an array of donuts, and anything else that would complete a binge. I was always concerned that others were looking at my cart in disgust. As I waited in line at the check-out counter, I would talk to those around me about my large family and how quickly they could eat. Everyone seemed to agree with me.

As I drove home, I would tear open packages and begin to shove food into my mouth. After I brought the groceries inside, the official binge would begin. I would eat so quickly that I rarely tasted anything. I would grab from one bag, then from a box. My glass of diet drink was emptied quickly and refilled. The more I drank during my binge, the easier the purging would be.

Empty containers would fill the kitchen counters and floor. They were scattered among the rest of the groceries. I would take the trash out of the trash bag, stuff the empty boxes in the bottom of the bag, and put the old trash back in. Sometimes the boxes were so numerous that hiding them wasn't enough. I would have to take the garbage to the dumpster so that the evidence of my binge wouldn't be discovered.

When it was time to purge, I was too familiar with the process. As I tied my hair back, I hated myself for what I was getting ready to do. I knew however, that if I didn't follow through, I would hate myself even more when I stepped on the scale. The violent heaving would make my heart race, my throat raw, and my eyes water. My cheeks were already swollen because of the irritation to my saliva glands. Although the process was disgusting, it had to be done correctly. Every small crumb had to be removed from my stomach. I would evaluate the contents in the commode to see if it looked like the same amount that I had eaten. Whole pieces of food were easily recognizable and I could usually distinguish between diet cola and small clots of blood.

Blood wasn't always present, but it's appearance terrified me. I was horrified to think that I might have to return to the hospital. John and I were having enough trouble paying for bills that were necessary. How could I justify paying the hospital and doctors for something that I had caused myself? Though I was scared, the fear was not enough to make me change my repulsive habit.

It was painful to feel large clumps of donuts and cookies coming up in exactly the same direction that they had gone down. I would often choke while trying to regurgitate because the large pieces would cover my windpipe. I would struggle to force air from my diaphragm to try and release the food into my mouth. From there, it would fall into the already full commode.

If John happened to be home when I returned from the store, I would unpack the bags without hesitation. Everything found it's proper place in the cabinet. If he left for any reason, the binge would begin. I would then have to clean up, purge, put my makeup back on, and race to the store. Once again, I would fill my cart. I would purchase everything that I had purged only minutes before. John had seen what I had in the bags, and it had to be in the cabinets when he returned. I would try to avoid store employees who had already seen me that day. They too might become suspicious.

I would rush home, put everything away, and start cooking supper. Often I would return to the commode to clean it thoroughly. Vomit would splash on the walls and the baseboards and I would painstakingly scrub them. I always felt that the more I cleaned, the dirtier my secret became.

Some things were miserable to regurgitate. Nuts, popcorn, and rice cakes had a grainy texture. They were harder to force back up and easier to come through the nasal cavities. I tried to avoid them.

If there was nothing suitable for a real binge available, I would create things. I would fill raw pie shells with cans of fruit, bake them for minutes, and call them a pie. I would put dry cocoa-mix on salted crackers and try to get pleasure from them. It didn't matter how things tasted. My goal was not to enjoy it going down or coming up. My job was simply to complete the process.

I would drive through fast food restaurants and order for two people. I would request two burgers, two fries, two drinks, and two desserts. The bag was usually empty by the time that I got home. All that remained was the purge.

Ice cream was the most comfortable thing to have during a binge. Coming back up, it was as smooth as silk. A friend once told me that she would order large shakes, drink them on the way home, then pull off of the road and vomit them back up into their original cup. She knew her stomach was empty when the cup was full. Ice cream from my stomach usually ended up in the sink. Since it didn't contain clumps, it didn't clog the drain.

Bulimia is not only life threatening, but it is very expensive. Parents have been known to report stolen money, only to discover their own child using the money to support the disease. I never understood why someone would waste money on cigarettes, alcohol, or drugs. However, my vision was clouded when it came to food. Since it is necessary for survival, I didn't see anything wrong with spending thirty dollars a day on things to flush down the commode.

Chapter 19

Wake Me from the Horror

I was given the opportunity to quit my job and attend school full time. I was very focused on my direction and immediately signed up for as many courses as the university would allow.

When John and I were married, I had a substantial savings account. However, years of my parents saving for my education had been used to purchase condos, furniture, and pay the electric bills. I was broke. My mother graciously offered to pay for my education. She was thrilled that I was headed in the right direction.

Because of my heavy class schedule and my continual struggle with my disease, I was getting very little sleep. The daily drive to the university was twenty-five minutes. During that time, I would often fall asleep. I would sip on diet colas, blast the radio, and roll down the windows. Nothing kept me awake. My body was screaming for help. As I would run into the gravel on the side of the road, I would be startled and jerk the car back.

Often I would be awakened by cars that noticed I was veering in their direction. I even was asleep long enough to dream on some occasions. I knew that I was not dealing well with pressures from school, my disease, and my marriage. I never actually considered suicide. However, I made it a habit to not wear my seat belt. I figured that if I had a wreck and died, that wouldn't be my fault. Obviously, God didn't have one angel watching over me, but an entire team!

The first thing I did when I arrived on campus was to visit the bookstore. There I would purchase twenty-five Atomic Fire Balls and a diet drink. That was to be the extent of my nutrition for the day. After hours of lectures and homework, I was ravenous.

I discovered an incredible donut shop three minutes from campus. Ironically, one of my professors owned it. I made it a habit to stop by everyday on my way home. I would order three lemon filled donuts, three large fried apple fritters, a few glazed donuts, and anything else that would complete the dozen. I would also order a large diet drink. I would talk to the guy behind the counter about the best way to freeze the pastries. I would also complain again about my large family and their food intake. I had a different story for each employee.

I would consume the entire dozen during my drive home. The diet drink helped to wash them down and I knew it would also help them come back up. Crumbs of donuts and pieces of glaze would cover the inside of my car. I didn't like things to be messy, but I was beyond caring. When the purge began, the donuts would be flushed in a matter of minutes. Although my stomach was distended and my body was exhausted, I would continue binging and purging until John came home. Spending the entire day without food had made it impossible for me to know when I was full. I simply knew that I couldn't stop eating. If I baked a cake at home, I would start eating it as soon as it was out of the pan. I would cut up what remained and put it on a crystal plate so that John wouldn't be able to tell how much of it was already missing. I would lie that I had given cookies to friends, or that they were burned and I had thrown them out. I was always devising more lies to hide my manipulative disease.

While I studied, I would always have things to munch on. Chips were a real favorite. They weren't great coming back up, but I did enjoy them going down.

After supper, I would clean any uneaten portions from pans and dishes by consuming them. I would also eat anything from John's plate that he hadn't eaten. It appeared that I was simply in the kitchen cleaning up. However, I was "feeding" my disease.

I felt that I was beyond repair. I was working tremendously hard at school, falling deeper into my disease, and getting emotionally farther away from my husband. Every time that I bent over to purge, I would vow that it was my last time. I would plead with God at night to make me well. I knew that I wasn't honoring my body which is a temple, but I didn't know how to stop myself. I would cry myself to sleep and promise to do better the next day. However, before the sun was up, I was back on my exercise bike repeating the vicious cycle.

John began to work with the local fire department. He was on duty for twenty-four hours, and off for forty-eight hours. During his off time, he worked for himself. The great amount of time that he was gone made it easier for me to relax about my secret. I could shop for food, and not have to restock the cabinets within minutes. I was less anxious about purging because I knew that he wouldn't come home and notice the stench in the air. I didn't have to reapply my make-up each time that I threw up. I was free to be a full-fledged bulimic. What a relief. I did enjoy making large meals and taking them to the fire hall to share with the others. I would get pleasure from their compliments. Although I usually ate with the crew, I would always find an excuse to leave early. On the way home, I would stop at a local fast food restaurant. I would order milkshakes and fried pies to gorge in the car.

For my birthday once, John bought me an ice cream cake. He had no idea what horrible things had happened to the first ice cream cake. It was mint chocolate-chip ice cream with chocolate cake. Since John was gone so much, he thought the cake was simply eaten over a period of days. He was wrong, it was consumed after a stressful day at the university.

John later decided to take some night classes as well. I was pleased with his decision. He was taking an emergency medical training course and doing very well. He was working hard and studying often. I was studying hard and purging often. Neither one of us was really aware of what was going on in the other one's life. We grew farther apart.

We decided to spend one night away and try to share some quality time together. I was a little uneasy about it because I was concerned about where I would purge. I assumed that if we were going to spend every moment together, the opportunity wouldn't be available. I was wrong. I found a way.

We enjoyed a nice rib dinner at a restaurant in the city. We both ate a hearty meal. We had reservations to stay in a fancy hotel. A few hours after we arrived, John became interested in a movie on TV. I tried to convince him to go downstairs and share the public hot tub with me. He was more interested in the movie. I put on my swimming suit and a cover-up. As I rode the elevator downstairs alone, I realized that something was terribly wrong with the picture. This was not how I had imagined our evening together. I located the bubbling tub, and then I located the bathroom. There, my expensive rib dinner met with it's fate. I was in a beautiful hotel throwing up into a plain ordinary commode. I spent the evening in the hot tub with a strange man. I wonder if his wife was upstairs watching TV? Maybe, she was purging her expensive dinner as well.

Chapter 20

Maybe There's Hope

My mother was surviving widowhood quite well. She built a beautiful new home, and was enjoying sharing time with friends. She had a job that kept her busy and she was managing on her own. Just when one least expects it, God throws one a curve ball. Sometimes one catches it and sometimes one just lets it slip on by. Mom caught this one dead center in her heart. She met a wonderful man. He was a widower as well. They were instantly compatible and enjoyed being together. We were all accepting of her relationship. The only thing that bothered us was that he lived four states away. It was hard for me to be happy for her when I knew that she might leave us.

Ultimately I decided that I would rather Mom be happy somewhere else than alone and in the same town as her children. I knew that I had to let her go.

There were so many things that I wanted to share with my mother before she left. I wanted her to know that I was unhappy in my three-year marriage. I wanted to reach out to her and tell her about my miserable illness. I wanted her to know that I feared that if she moved away, she would die and I wouldn't be there for her either. I wanted her to know that I felt like my life was becoming completely unraveled. Instead, I smiled and helped her make wonderful wedding plans. I had to be strong for her.

I was Mom's maid of honor. We found a beautiful and elegant dress for me to wear. The wedding was going to be on her new deck that surrounded the swimming pool. Flowers would be floating on the top of the softly tinted water. A huge tent was erected to shield guests from the blazing sun. It was to be a glorious affair.

When Mom and I purchased my dress, it fit perfectly. On the day of her wedding, the size 8/9 dress had to be pinned to my body. Because of all the emotional turmoil that I was under, I was losing more weight rapidly. No one seemed concerned, they simply complemented me on my beautiful attire. When I look back at pictures from that event, I realize that I was desperately ill. My waist was tiny, but my face was swollen. It's too bad that no one knew the warning signs because I was exhibiting so many of them.

As John and I spent less time together, we became less sensitive to each other. One particular Friday night, we made it a point to be together. He unexpectedly got called into work at the fire hall for a few hours. We decided to wait and eat pizza when he got home and simply relax on the couch. I waited for his return and actually looked forward to our quiet evening. When John walked through the door, he handed me a large pizza box. I could tell by the way it felt that it wasn't full and that the pizza had to be cold. "What's this?" I said. "Oh," he replied, "we ordered pizza at the station. This is what is left." He turned on the television and sat down in his favorite chair. "I want to see the rest of this movie," he said. I was furious. I had waited all night for his return. I had not eaten because we were going to do that together. For once I wanted to be with him, and he could have cared less about my presence in the room. I stormed out of the house without saying a word.

As quickly as I could I ran to my car. I locked the doors as soon as I sat inside. I was certain that he wouldn't come after me, but I didn't want him to try and coax me out. I stuck the key in the ignition and pumped the gas as rapidly as I could. I had to get away! I wanted to get away from him, from our marriage, from myself. I drove quickly and with only one destination in mind.

I ended up at my favorite frozen yogurt shop. I ordered the largest thing they had to offer and ate it in my car. I didn't want anyone to see me as I shoved spoonfuls of raspberry yogurt in my mouth without taking the time to wipe my face. I didn't want them to see me taking out my anger on this delectable treat. I didn't want anyone to see that I was out of control. On the way home, I stopped at the nearby McDonald's and purged my raspberry yogurt with sprinkles in a waffle cone. The purge didn't make me feel the slightest bit better; however, at least I had control over that poor yogurt. God knows that I had no control over my miserable life.

School was hectic, John was very busy, and I was extremely lonely. I stopped by the bank one sunny morning on my way to the university. It was there that I saw the most magnificent sight. Walking up the bank steps wearing his coaching jacket and his infamous polyester pants was Coach Larry Watkins. I hadn't seen his smile nor heard his voice since graduation four years earlier. All of the mint chocolate chip ice cream cakes in the world couldn't make me as happy as I was at that moment. As I approached him unsuspectingly, my heart was racing and my palms were sweating. For a second, I wondered if he would be happy to see me. I wondered if I looked presentable. I wondered if he would even remember me. With one glance, my fears were erased. We embraced on the sidewalk and his warm touch soothed me like nothing had in years. While we talked, time stood still. The flowers on the walkway smelled sweeter and the sun was warmer on my back. God had thrown me a curve ball and I was determined not to let it slip away. I didn't know where this extraordinary feeling was coming from nor how long it would last. However, it was nice to know that somewhere deep inside me I could still feel this good. Maybe there was hope.

Chapter 21

A Mother's Tender Touch

Health class was a required course for all education majors at my university. As with all of my classes, I was doing well and studying hard. I was taught how to perform CPR. I was taught how to bandage bleeding wounds. I was even taught how to prepare a proper first aid kit. The one thing that I wasn't taught was how to make myself well. The topic of eating disorders was covered, but only briefly. There was no class discussion with the lesson and no ideas on how to manage the problem.

I became very concerned about my own health when we discussed problems that can occur in the heart. I was often experiencing complete numbness on either side of my body. My fingers would tingle, and my toes would become immobile. I could feel my erratic heart beat often and I would break into a sweat while remaining still in my seat. The symptoms scared me and I was afraid that I might meet with the same fate as my father.

I scheduled a visit with a doctor and waited for my secret to be discovered. The doctor checked my heart rate. He weighed me and also checked my blood pressure. Within a matter of minutes, he concluded that I was fine. "Are you under any stress?" he asked.

I chuckled, "Well, I am working very hard in school and training to maintain an impossible grade average."

"That's your problem," he said. "You just have too many things on your mind. Stress can manifest itself in various ways." He left the room.

That was it. Stress was his diagnosis. Maybe if I told him that I exercised for hours, threw up on the average of ten times a day, and only had one bowel movement a month, he would have done further tests. It wasn't his fault that I didn't volunteer this information. However, it was his job to do a detailed examination. Even though I was terrified of being discovered, I was desperately wanting someone to help me. I thought that coming to his office was a huge step. I had been let down again.

When one heaves violently one's heart rate increases. My purging was so often that my heart was struggling to maintain a perfect balance. I was later diagnosed as being on the verge of suffering from cardiac arrest.

I mentioned to John that I had visited the doctor. I told him all about my symptoms and my fears. I told him everything except the fact that I was still constantly battling my disease. Why couldn't someone see through me? Why couldn't they tell that I had a very severe problem? John accepted the diagnosis of stress and remained unconcerned. Maybe he was scared. Maybe he was uninformed. Maybe he didn't care.

In the very pit of my soul, I was terrified. I felt like I was dangling from a string over a blazing fire. At any moment I could snap the string and I would plummet into the flames. I would be immediately destroyed and no one would notice my disappearance. I was slowly disappearing before all of my friends and family anyway and no one was trying to pull me up. At times I thought that my life could have a tiny purpose, but those moments were rare. Countless hours were wasted telling myself how completely worthless I was. I was spinning furiously in circles on the inside and was smiling brightly on the outside.

I took a chance and got in touch with Coach over the phone. He immediately made me feel a bit calmer inside. His demeanor and his sense of humor brought a freshness to my life where only the stale taste of vomit had been. Our conversations became frequent. John was often gone at night and Coach and I would spend hours on the phone. He began to fill in emotional gaps that had been vacant for years. I could visualize his sparkling eyes every time we would share laughter. I would watch the sun go down through the trees while we talked and see its reflection in the glass as it made its way back up. Time was not important while we tried to recapture all of the moments that we had missed during the last four years.

Coach gave me a sense that I did matter. He seemed to enjoy our conversations and seemed to care about me. He would be the first to ask me how I had done on a test during the day and the first to recognize disappointment in my voice. He was inside of my head and he was directing my heart.

On the day that I had taken my wedding vows, I had taken them seriously. However, words are easy to repeat. I discovered over a period of three years that planning a wedding was easy; living a marriage takes a lot of work from two willing partners. I was no longer willing to work.

The emotions that came over me the day that John emptied out our home are indescribable. Three years earlier, we were selecting china and furniture. Now we were fighting over them. Things that had meant absolutely nothing to him during our marriage were suddenly his treasured items. I let go of almost everything that we had gotten together because I simply wanted to let go of him. I returned from school one day to find our condo almost completely empty. There were books scattered on the floor that had been on shelves the night before. There were socks in a box that had been kept in a beautiful antique chest. There were sheets where our bed had been. Although I had initiated the divorce, I still felt like I had been violated. It wasn't John's fault. Everything that he took belonged to him. However, the reality of the separation came to light only with the reality of my empty condo. I slept on the couch and tried to keep my clothes sorted neatly in their boxes. Although I was without material things, I slowly began to piece myself back together. With each new day, I would try to look myself in the mirror and identify one positive quality. Sometimes I would stand and battle with my own mind. One part of my brain would suggest that maybe I had nice skin and the other part would deny that I was worthy of life. It was often a struggle, but I was beginning to realize that maybe, just maybe, there was a reason that my disease had brought me this far without removing the breath from my body or the fight from my spirit.

I finally told my mother about my battle with bulimia. She immediately embraced my thinning body and stroked my hair. In her arms I felt safe. I knew that my mommy could help me. Now that she knew about my problem, I could begin to reach out for help. As a child, I had always thought that my parents could do anything. With each stroke of her warm hand, those feelings returned. I was very fortunate. My mother began to research my disease and to do anything that she could to let me know that she was on my side. Some parents turn away from their children's problems because they are hard to understand or to deal with. God gave me a mother who was ready and willing to join me in my struggle. She purchased a small book titled *Coping with Bulimia*. It was a little book but an enormous gesture. She helped me find a counselor and insisted on paying for my sessions. She wanted to do all that she could and more.

I was hired as a teacher immediately out of school. I was thrilled with my position and felt fortunate to finally be doing what I had dreamed of for a lifetime. I was conscientious about my position and strived to be the best teacher that I could be. I felt honored to take tiny minds and fill them with information. Everything was new and wonderful to my students. We were a great team. They needed my knowledge and I needed their innocence.

One day when I returned home from work, I found a large package leaning against my front door. Inside the heavy box I found a beautiful, colorful sweater. The card attached read, "This is your *Yea, I didn't throw up today* sweater." It was a weird reason to celebrate, but my mother knew that each day in recovery was significant. She was reaching out to me across the miles that separated us physically.

Chapter 22

Learning to Trust

From the moment that she knew about my disease, my mother knew that she had an important job to do. I had reached a point that I no longer cared about myself; she cared about me enough for both of us. I had spent eleven years perfecting my disease. I had mastered my manipulation. I was suffering so drastically that my repulsive actions no longer disgusted me. My struggle had become the focus of my life, and it was difficult to see beyond its horrid effects. I had lost all perception of reality and thought that everyone else based my self-worth on my figure. With the help of my mother, my counselor, Larry Watkins, and my God, I very gradually began to turn my thinking around.

When I trusted Larry with my secret, I was relieved with his reaction. He didn't question me. He didn't turn from me. He simply held me. His warmth gave me energy. It gave me a reason to strive to be well. I knew that I had to get better for myself, but he gave me incentive. He wanted me around and that was important to me. If he wanted me, then I must be worth something.

My counselor directed me to a clinic in Nashville. I immediately knew that I had found a place that both my mind and body could heal. It was scary to think that I would ultimately have to disclose my years of manipulation in order to completely heal. The great thing was that I also realized that I was worth healing.

The old brick building where my healing began was located in downtown Nashville. The exterior of the building was beautiful. It was surrounded by an iron gate and it loomed over the local park. To see the beautiful bricks from the outside, one could never realize what barriers the patients inside had built around themselves.

During my first visit to Park West Eating Disorders Clinic, I sat with another girl in the waiting room. I felt like she was uncomfortable. I assumed that she expected me to be wondering about her. I sensed her fear and tried to make conversation. I wasn't sure what to talk to her about so I talked about something that was close to me. "Do you think that it's best to brush your teeth after you purge or just let the saliva balance out the acid in your mouth?" "What?" she said. I repeated my question. She twisted nervously in her chair and I instantly realized that I had asked the wrong question. I was only trying to make her feel comfortable. I returned to looking at my magazine and waited for my name to be called.

I was a member in a group therapy setting. The room where we met was at the top of the building. It was a tiny space that was filled with different people and different problems. Boxes of Kleenex could be found in every corner and stuffed animals were available for hugging. There was one couch and several chairs. We entered the group strangers but emerged victorious friends.

One night each week we would meet. We would spend an hour crying, holding hands, laughing, encouraging. We needed each other and we were thankful to have found others who truly understood our struggle.

The most enjoyable person that I met in therapy was a beautiful woman named Tamara. She was very tall and had long, dark hair. Before I realized how special Tamara was on the inside, I observed Tamara from the outside. Her blue spidery veins were easily visible on her spindly arms. Her hair had no shine and her cheekbones were protruding from her pale face. Her smile was brilliant but weak. She was obviously once beautiful, but beauty had given way to her sickness.

Tamara and I instantly bonded. She was able to talk about her struggle with anorexia, but was quick to try and offer friendly advice to others. She could tell when I wanted to cry and would pat my back as I held in the tears. She had a gift for boosting my spirits and showing me reasons to continue with my healing. When I would want to give up, she would insist that I push forward.

Tamara, like everyone else in the group, was literally dying to be thin. She had moved to Nashville to become a performer, yet focused all of her time and energy on her disease. She wouldn't go out with friends for fear of being asked to have pizza or any other forbidden food. With Tamara, every food was forbidden. She would spend hours working out at the YMCA and hours running around her block. She would get bruises from sitting in the tub because she had no fat to cushion her. She said that anorexia was "a sickness from the chin up." I thought that Tamara was very special and didn't understand why she couldn't see that about herself.

Therapy was a real blessing for me. With each session I would open up a little more. I was slowly peeling away my shell and discovering who I really was. I felt like I was in a safe place and I knew that my new friends could relate to how I was feeling.

Many years of struggling with bulimia had made me develop incredibly bad habits. I had vomited so much and so often that my digestive system was not functioning properly. During one of my final purges, I regurgitated a meal that I had eaten twenty-four hours earlier. It was completely undigested.

Larry once commented about an awful smell in the room. When he began to search for its origin, he discovered that the terrible stench was coming from my hair. I had purged earlier, and it had become matted in my hair. I was unaware of it, and had become used to the smell. He gently let me know that the stench repulsed him. However, he also assured me that I didn't.

Ham sandwiches, chips, and bottled water slowly nursed me back to health. I would often spend time with Larry and this is what he would feed me. It might not have been food that a nutritionist would order, but it was food that remained in my system. With these ingredients, my body slowly learned how to digest food again.

Larry had two wonderful boys, Zack and Zeke. They both attended school where I taught and I took an instant liking to them. They learned quickly that they could come to me if they were out of ice cream money or if they needed something for their class. I think they liked me and they liked the fact that I was there to help them when they needed it. Larry was a wonderful father. He could roll around on the ground with his boys, yet gently stroke them when they needed comforting. He wasn't caught up with being a man, but with being an individual. I loved him for so many reasons.

On January 16, 1990, we were married at the local courthouse. That night we ate chicken on the floor by candlelight. The next day I went to work and he went to the dentist. I was Mrs. Larry Watkins. The ceremony wasn't eventful, but I knew that our lifetime together would most definitely be.

Chapter 23

Delicate Second Chances

The following words were what I had been screaming out for years. My disease had started at the age of thirteen, but my feelings of insecurity and unworthiness began when I was so tiny. When my counselor gave me this writing from Charles Whitfield's *Healing the Child Within* (Health Communications, Inc.: Deerfield Beach, Florida, 1987), I felt like someone had opened my soul and completely exposed it. The author was writing about me. This had to be written for me. This was *me*! I gave a copy of it to Larry, and we both grew from it.

Please Hear What I'm Not Saying

Don't be fooled by me.
Don't be fooled by the face I wear.
For I wear a mask, a thousand masks,
masks that I'm afraid to take off,
and none of them is me.
Pretending is an art that's second nature with me,
but don't be fooled,
for God's sake don't be fooled.
I give you the impression that I am secure,
that all is sunny and unruffled with me, within as well
    as without,
that confidence is my name and coolness my game,
that the water's calm and I'm in command,
and that I need no one.
But don't believe me.
My surface may seem smooth but my surface is my mask,
every-varying and ever-concealing.

Beneath lies no complacence.
Beneath lies confusion, and fear, and aloneness.
But I hide this. I don't want anybody to know it.
I panic at the thought of my weakness and fear being
　　exposed.
That's why I frantically create a mask to hide behind,
a nonchalant sophisticated facade,
to help me pretend,
to shield me from the glance that knows.
But such a glance is precisely my salvation. My only hope.
　　And I know it.
That is, if it's followed by acceptance,
if it's followed by love.
It's the only thing that can liberate me from myself,
from my own self-built prison walls,
from the barriers I so painstakingly erect.
It's the only thing that will assure me of what I can't
　　assure myself,
that I'm really worth something.
But I don't tell you this. I don't dare. I'm afraid to.
I'm afraid your glance will not be followed by acceptance,
will not be followed by love.
I'm afraid you'll think less of me, that you'll laugh,
and your laugh would kill me.
I'm afraid that deep-down I'm nothing, that I'm just no
　　good,
and that you will see this and reject me.
So I play my game, my desperate pretending game,
with a facade of assurance without
and a trembling child within.
So begins the glittering but empty parade of masks,
and my life becomes a front.
I idly chatter to you in the suave tones of surface talk.
I tell you everything that's really nothing,
and nothing of what's everything,
of what's crying within me.
So when I'm going through my routine
do not be fooled by what I'm saying.
Please listen carefully and try to hear what I'm not saying,
what I'd like to be able to say,

what for survival I need to say,
but what I can't say.
I don't like to hide.
I don't like to play superficial phony games.
I want to stop playing them.
I want to be genuine and spontaneous and me,
but you've got to help me.
You've got to hold out your hand
even when that's the last thing I seem to want.
Only you can wipe away from my eyes the blank stare of
    the breathing dead.
Only you can call me into aliveness.
Each time you're kind, and gentle, and encouraging,
each time you try to understand because you really care,
my heart begins to grow wings,
very small wings,
very feeble wings,
but wings!
With your power to touch me into feeling
you can breathe life into me.
I want you to know that.
I want you to know how important you are to me,
how you can be a creator—an honest-to-God creator—
of the person that is me
if you choose to.
You alone can break down the wall behind which I tremble,
you alone can remove my mask,
you alone can release me from my shadow-world of panic
    and uncertainty, from my lonely prison,
if you choose to.
Please choose to. Do not pass me by.
It will not be easy for you.
A long conviction of worthlessness builds strong walls.
The nearer you approach to me
the blinder I may strike back.
It's irrational, but despite what the books say about man,
often I am irrational.
I fight against the very thing that I cry out for.
But I am told that love is stronger than strong walls,
and in this lies my hope.

Please try to beat down those walls
with firm hands
but with gentle hands
for a child is very sensitive.

Who am I, you may wonder?
I am someone you know very well.
For I am every man you meet
and I am every woman you meet.

Every step in my recovery was significant. I was able to identify situations that could possibly lead to a binge and avoid them. One morning after Valentine's Day, I asked Larry to take all of my goodies from my students to work with him. I wasn't comfortable having them around. Without a frown, a look of concern, nor a look of dismay, he loaded them into his car. If they were gone, I was safe.

Habits that have been practiced for many years are hard to change. My recovery was a daily process. However, small steps forward led to climbing over major hurdles. I was thrilled when I noticed one night that I was the only member in our therapy group that had her shirt tucked in. I took that to mean that I was beginning to feel better about myself. People with eating disorders try to conceal their bodies. I was starting to reveal mine. During my recovery, I did gain several pounds. It was a struggle to deal with, but I knew that my health was more important than the numbers on the scale. Eventually with proper diet and exercise, I lost the weight. It simply took my body a little while to completely adjust to having three normal meals a day.

I once found a half-eaten bag of M&M's that I had hidden. I had forgotten about them and discovered them tucked away in my closet. I knew that I was a step closer to wellness. For a bulimic to forget about food is completely uncommon. I had done it and was certain that I was going to be okay.

Larry and I wanted children that could grow up with the boys. We were both determined to have a family. Although he had a vasectomy ten years earlier, we prayed, gave the doctor five thousand dollars, and asked to have his operation reversed. Almost one year from that date, we gave birth to a healthy baby boy. As I held him in my hands for the first time, I immediately realized that I could have easily damaged my body so tremendously that this precious moment might not have been possible. In my quest to be thin, I could have given up my chances for having children. I rubbed his soft skin and kissed his tiny face. He was a supreme blessing. Baker Douglas Watkins had beaten the odds and become the ultimate product of our steadfast love for each other.

As I watched him sleep on Larry's chest my heart wept. With each breath from Larry, his tiny body would move. He was a miracle and he was ours. We charted his progress daily and thought that nothing could make us happier. We were wrong.

Sixteen months later, God blessed us with an incredible daughter. I watched Baker rub her tiny face and say "baby" in his soft voice. I watched Larry beam as he caressed her and held her closely. I felt a bond like no other as she got her nourishment from me. Her small, fragile face gently receiving milk from my breasts. How had all of this happened?

Three years earlier, I was questioning whether or not I was worthy of living. Now I was giving life. My husband had guided me through many terrible storms and I was able to hold and love our children as a result of my healing. Molly Katherine Watkins was a gift and an angel rolled into one package. Her eyes danced as she watched her three brothers play. They beamed with pride when they would tell friends that they had a sister. The six of us were a real family. We were a real, healthy, vibrant family.

Chapter 24

It's a Wonderful Life

Although I haven't experienced binging and purging in over four years, I am not completely recovered. I will never be completely recovered. There are still days when I have a hard time looking at myself and finding something positive. However, if I can't find it in myself, I can find it all around me. My children are a reflection of my happiness. They cause me to look even closer at myself and discover what an incredible life I have and that I am happy inside.

I am very aware that it would be easy for me to develop bad habits again. I daily think about my body, yet quickly remind myself that I am unique and that society's perception of beautiful is not mine. If my words falter, Larry directs my thinking onto the proper path.

We truly think that we are the product of a miracle. We don't believe that God intended for us to be divorced, bulimic, or lonely, but we are certain that he planned for us to be together. We accept everyday as a gift because we feel so fortunate to be together. We are not proud that we had failed marriages, but the failures make it possible for us to appreciate the successes in our relationship. We take nothing for granted.

Our life together is wonderful. We have four incredible children. We have each other. We have God. He is always there to guide us when we think we're okay, and love us when we think we can't go any further.

I still exercise daily, but in moderation. The scale has a place in my home, but it does not rule my head. I don't stock our house with cookies and cakes, but an occasional treat is mandatory. I am twenty-eight years old and realize that I will never be able to diet again. Restriction sets me up for disaster. For me, this is not a sign of weakness, but of strength. I work on setting good examples for my children concerning food. Food is not taken away as punishment nor is it given as a reward. It's only purpose is to nourish the body. I want my children to know that they are beautiful. When Larry and I rest their tiny heads on their pillows each night, we say a little prayer. Then we think of something great they did that day, and tell them how special they are. We work at letting them know that they are unique. The last thing they hear each night is something that makes them feel good about themselves. Though small, the smiles on their faces prove to us that they love the praise.

The greatest thing that I have discovered is that I do matter and that I am important. I recently spoke to a group of teenagers about my struggle with the terrible disease bulimia. I watched their faces turn away in disgust. I heard them moan as they became repulsed. I saw the tears as they wiped their faces dry. Most importantly, I saw a glimmer of hope in eyes where I believe the disease is already striking.

I'm not proud of my years of anguish. However, I am exhilarated knowing that I can recognize my faults without wanting to harm myself. I am thankful that I am healthy and that I am alive.

My mother has always told me that as a child I gravitated to stories about people overcoming adversity. Ironically, my story is that same kind of example. With the grace of God, love from my family, and strength from somewhere within, I know that I will be okay. My heart is peaceful and my happiness is truly genuine.

Finding a Therapist and Remaining in Therapy

Suggestions from the National Association of Anorexia Nervosa and Associated Disorders (ANAD)

Some of the therapists ANAD lists certainly are familiar with anorexia nervosa and treat it. Other therapists may not be treating anorexia but, hopefully, can direct you to someone who does.

Since there are many philosophies concerning the treatment of anorexia nervosa and many personality differences in both patients and therapists, ANAD strongly recommends that you explore the suitability of the therapist from a very personal standpoint to ensure finding the therapist who can work best with you or you and your family.

ANAD feels that your best approach is to familiarize yourself, through reading, with all the phases of anorexia and the treatment approaches and then select a therapist who makes the most sense for your particular circumstances.

The therapist's rapport with an individual (and her family, if this applies), and confidence in the proposed treatment approach are important considerations.

If the symptoms appear to you to be the symptoms of anorexia nervosa or bulimia but the therapist suggests that no problem exists, or recommends that the problem can be handled by the individual without treatment, do not hesitate to ask for another opinion.

Nor should one hesitate to seek another therapist if, after a reasonable time, no progress is evident. Before changing therapists this should be discussed with the present therapist. Having considered the therapist's views one can make a more informed decision on changing or not changing therapists.

If the fees are too high, check local (state/county) mental health facilities or private welfare agencies that operate on a sliding scale. Any therapist who is willing to work with an anorexic on the problems of low self-esteem, depression, anxiety, and guilt should produce some positive results providing a good therapeutic relationship has been established.

ANAD can only suggest names of therapists but cannot be responsible for the success or failure of their treatment. We will be glad to provide them with our bibliography, share our experience, or help in any way that we can.

ANAD has a listing of qualified persons to provide assistance in each state. For more information, contact ANAD, Box 7, Highland Park, IL   60035, (708) 831-3438.